Tiny Plays for Ireland

TINY PLAYS FOR IRELAND

NEW ISLAND

TINY PLAYS FOR IRELAND
First published 2013
by New Island
2 Brookside
Dundrum Road
Dublin 14

www.newisland.ie

PRINT ISBN: 978-1-84840-214-0
EPUB ISBN: 978-1-84840-215-7
MOBI ISBN: 978-1-84840-216-4

Typeset by JM InfoTech INDIA
Cover design by David Darcy
Printed by TJ International Ltd, Padstow, Cornwall

New Island received financial assistance from
The Arts Council (An Comhairle Ealaíon), Dublin, Ireland

10 9 8 7 6 5 4 3 2 1

Contents

'Fishamble puts electricity in the national grid of dreams.'
Sebastian Barry

'In order to keep vibrant, theatre requires constant transfusions of new plays. This life-providing role is fulfilled enthusiastically and with wonderful results by Fishamble. Without them, Irish theatre would be anaemic.'
Brian Friel

About Fishamble:
The New Play Company

Fishamble is an award-winning, internationally acclaimed company, dedicated to the discovery, development and production of new work for the Irish stage. During 2013, Fishamble is celebrating its 25th birthday. Over the past 25 years, the Company has produced 131 new plays, including 42 stand alone plays and 89 short plays as part of longer works, by first-time and established playwrights. Fishamble is delighted that, in its 25th year, its body of work will be archived in Ireland by the National Library of Ireland, and in the U.S. by the University of Notre Dame.

Fishamble is committed to touring its work to audiences throughout Ireland and internationally, and typically presents approximately 200 performances of its plays in 80 venues per year. Fishamble has brought its productions to audiences in all parts of Ireland, as well as to England, Scotland, USA, Canada, Australia, Bulgaria, Romania, Turkey, France, Germany, Iceland, Croatia and the Czech Republic.

Fishamble's awards include Fringe First Awards, Herald Angel Awards, Argus Angel Awards, *Irish Times* Theatre Awards, 1st Irish Awards and, for many of its first-time playwrights, Stewart Parker Trust Awards.

Fishamble is at the heart of new writing for theatre in Ireland, not just through its productions, but through its extensive programme of training, development and mentoring schemes. Each year, Fishamble supports 60 per cent of the writers of all new plays produced on the island of Ireland, approximately 50 plays per year. This happens in a variety of ways; for instance, Fishamble supports:

- **the public** through an ongoing range of playwriting courses in Dublin and off-site for literary and arts festivals nationwide;
- **playwrights and theatre companies** through The New Play Clinic, which develops new plays planned for production by theatre artists and companies, and the annual Fishamble New Writing Award at Dublin Fringe;
- **actors** through its Show in a Bag programme, which creates and showcases new plays for actors, in association with the Irish Theatre Institute and Dublin Fringe;
- **students** through work in association with TCD, NUIG, NUIM, IES, DIT, and as Theatre Company in Association at UCD Drama Studies Centre;
- **emerging artists** through mentoring schemes in association with venues and local authorities, for playwrights and directors.

Fishamble is funded by the Arts Council and Dublin City Council.

Its international touring is supported by Culture Ireland.

Fishamble Staff

Artistic Director   Jim Culleton
General Manager   Marketa Dowling
Literary Manager   Gavin Kostick

About Fishamble: The New Play Company

Fishamble Board: Tania Banotti, Caroline Cullen, Peter Finnegan, Vincent O'Doherty, Andrew Parkes, Brendan Rice.

Fishamble: The New Play Company
Shamrock Chambers
1/2 Eustace Street
Dublin 2
Ireland
Tel: +353–1-670 4018, fax: +353–1-670 4019

email: info@fishamble.com
www.fishamble.com
www.facebook.com/fishamble
www.twitter.com/fishamble

Previous Productions of New Plays

2012
Tiny Plays for Ireland by 25 writers
Silent by Pat Kinevane (revival)
Mainstream by Rosaleen McDonagh (script-in-hand)
The Great Goat Bubble by Julian Gough*
The Wheelchair on My Face by Sonya Kelly*
Forgotten by Pat Kinevane (revival)

2011
Silent by Pat Kinevane
The End of the Road by Gavin Kostick
The Pride of Parnell Street by Sebastian Barry (revival)
Forgotten by Pat Kinevane (revival)
The Music of Ghost Light by Joseph O'Connor
Noah and the Tower Flower by Seán McLoughlin (revival)

2010
Big Ole Piece of Cake by Seán McLoughlin
Turning Point by John Austin Connolly, Steve Daunt*, Stephen
Kennedy and Rosaleen McDonagh
Forgotten (revival) by Pat Kinevane

2009
Strandline by Abbie Spallen
The Pride of Parnell Street by Sebastian Barry (revival)
Forgotten by Pat Kinevane (revival)
Handel's Crossing by Joseph O'Connor
Noah and the Tower Flower by Seán McLoughlin (revival)

Previous Productions of New Plays

2008
Forgotten by Pat Kinevane (revival)
The Pride of Parnell Street by Sebastian Barry (revival)
Rank by Robert Massey

2007
The Pride of Parnell Street by Sebastian Barry
Noah and the Tower Flower by Seán McLoughlin*
Forgotten by Pat Kinevane

2006
Monged by Gary Duggan (revival)
Whereabouts – a series of short, site-specific plays by Shane
Carr*, John Cronin*, John Grogan*, Louise Lowe, Belinda
McKeon*, Colin Murphy*, Anna Newell*, Jack Olohan*, Jody
O'Neill*, Tom Swift and Jacqueline Strawbridge*
Forgotten by Pat Kinevane (work-in-progress)
The Gist of It by Rodney Lee*

2005
Monged by Gary Duggan*
She Was Wearing … by Sebastian Barry, Maeve Binchy, Dermot
Bolger, Michael Collins, Stella Feehily, Rosalind Haslett,
Róisín Ingle*, Marian Keyes* and Gavin Kostick

2004
Pilgrims in the Park by Jim O'Hanlon
Tadhg Stray Wandered In by Michael Collins

2003
Handel's Crossing by Joseph O'Connor, *The Medusa* by Gavin
Kostick, *Chaste Diana* by Michael West and *Sweet Bitter* by
Stella Feehily (a season of radio plays)

Shorts by Dawn Bradfield*, Aino Dubrawsky*, Simon O'Gorman*, Ciara Considine*, Tina Reilly*, Mary Portser, Colm Maher*, James Heaney*, Tara Dairman*, Lorraine McArdle*, Talaya Delaney*, Ger Gleeson*, Stella Feehily* and Bryan Delaney*
The Buddhist of Castleknock by Jim O'Hanlon (revival)

2002
Contact by Jeff Pitcher and Gavin Kostick
The Buddhist of Castleknock by Jim O'Hanlon*
Still by Rosalind Haslett*

2001
The Carnival King by Ian Kilroy*
Wired to the Moon by Maeve Binchy, adapted by Jim Culleton

2000
Y2K Festival: *Consenting Adults* by Dermot Bolger, *Dreamframe* by Deirdre Hines, *Moonlight and Music* by Jennifer Johnston, *The Great Jubilee* by Nicholas Kelly*, *Doom Raider* by Gavin Kostick, *Tea Set* by Gina Moxley

1999
The Plains of Enna by Pat Kinevane
True Believers by Joseph O'Connor

1998
The Nun's Wood by Pat Kinevane*
1997
From Both Hips by Mark O'Rowe*

1996
The Flesh Addict by Gavin Kostick

Previous Productions of New Plays

1995
Sardines by Michael West
Red Roses and Petrol by Joseph O'Connor*

1994
Jack Ketch's Gallows Jig by Gavin Kostick

1993
Buffalo Bill Has Gone to Alaska by Colin Teevan
The Ash Fire by Gavin Kostick (revival)

1992
The Ash Fire by Gavin Kostick*
The Tender Trap by Michael West

1991
Howling Moons/Silent Sons by Deirdre Hines*
This Love Thing by Marina Carr

1990
Don Juan by Michael West
* denotes first play by a new playwright as part of *Fishamble Firsts*

New plays are under commission from Sebastian Barry, Gavin Kostick, Gina Moxley, Seán McLoughlin, Pat Kinevane, Deirdre Kinahan, Donal O'Kelly, Colin Murphy and Rosaleen McDonagh.

Acknowledgements

Fishamble wishes to thank the following Friends of Fishamble for their invaluable support:

Brian Friel, Alan and Caroline Gray, Noelle Maguire and Manus McClafferty, Colum McCann, Vincent O'Doherty, Andrew and Delyth Parkes, Lisa Cook and Richard Cook, David and Veronica Rowe, Patrick and Mo Sutton. Thank you to all who do not wish to be credited.

Fishamble is delighted to present this very special new production, which has been developed in partnership with *The Irish Times* and the Irish Copyright Licensing Agency. Special thanks to: David Parnell and all at the Arts Council, Gerry Smyth, Shane Hegarty, Fintan O'Toole and all at *The Irish Times*; Samantha Holmes and all at the Irish Copyright Licensing Agency; Cian O'Brien, Niamh O'Donnell, Melanie Wright, Joseph Collins and all at the Project Arts Centre; Eoin Purcell and all at New Island Books; and all those who have helped Fishamble with the production since this publication went to print.

Introduction

Fishamble: The New Play Company is always searching for, and developing, plays that capture contemporary times. In order to reflect on the country's current situation, we decided to put our trust in the Irish public and launched a national call for submissions, through *The Irish Times*, for tiny plays to add to the debate about where Ireland is, and where the country is going. We asked people to consider what they could achieve with three or four minutes of stage time, what issues they felt needed to be addressed, and what characters they wanted to bring to life on stage. We commissioned plays by some of Ireland's top writers to start the project, and a selection of these were published in *The Irish Times* to share how some writers had dealt with the challenge of writing a 600-word play that captured a glimpse, moment or encounter of contemporary relevance.

We were thrilled with the response, receiving over 1,700 tiny plays, indicating how deeply the Irish public feels about the issues explored in the plays and the need to express them. In fact, the word count of all the plays submitted amounts to more than double that of *War and Peace,* or four times that of *Lord of the Rings*! We received plays about all aspects of life, from every county on the island of Ireland, as well as from over a dozen other countries. The youngest playwright was 7 years of age; the oldest was 81.

The plays were full of passion, whether it was expressing anger at Ireland's current economic situation, sadness at instances of social injustice, or joy at an expression of love in an ordinary, everyday encounter. Writers were interested, of course, in perennial social issues including homelessness, bereavement, politics and the recession, but also in other, less expected areas. Reading all the plays gave us a very real, immediate insight into what the Irish public wanted to say about contemporary life. It was a privilege to read such a range of work and to get a picture of the ideas that people from all over the country, and outside it, decided to express through their tiny plays. We are particularly pleased that so many people, whether their play was chosen for production or not, remarked that it had been a great catalyst to write a play and that it had given them the confidence and motivation to work on another, more substantial work.

Our next challenge was to work out how to do justice to the level of creativity and interest that the project generated. The number of plays that seemed complete and satisfying, with a turning point, a moment of discovery, or a character progression, that seemed to be just right for the short timeframe of the play, was very impressive. So we decided to double the number of plays we would produce, and mount two separate productions – one production of 25 tiny plays in Project Arts Centre in March 2012 and another production of a different 25 plays in March 2013.

The plays chosen from those submitted depict events that include: a woman singing to her husband as they dance on a carpet of unpaid bills; two old friends milking cows by hand during a power cut; a whole lifetime condensed into four minutes; a mother and her teenage son arguing over a sexist billboard at a Dart station; an outrageous sexual encounter between two financial asset managers; a man discovering naked photographs of his mother when clearing out the attic;

a teenager waiting on a platform for a train to arrive in four minutes as he contemplates committing suicide.

This last play is one of a total of 119 submissions which were written by young people – some of these were chosen for the full productions and Fishamble presented a free public reading of a selection of others, to share the thoughts and ideas of people under 18 years of age with the public. This was part of a larger programme of free debates and discussions accompanying the productions.

Once the plays were chosen, we needed to decide which plays would be part of each production and in what order they would be performed, so that the audience would have a unified and satisfying experience, hopefully. The running order of plays in production began with those set in early morning, progressing through the day, to night, back to early morning again. This hopefully allowed the action to progress through a 24-hour cycle, so a play in Dáil Éireann late at night, or following the evening news, takes place later in the production than a play with a separated father collecting his child from school, or two teenagers waiting outside the principal's office following a violent incident.

The productions were staged in the round, so the theatre resembled a mini sports arena, or political forum. The set resembled two paths intersecting, to create a sense of plays happening 'at the crossroads'. While the audience witnessed 25 plays, we were keen to avoid 24 scene changes, so the set allowed plays to exist in their own right, but also to help the momentum of the overall production.

On the first morning of rehearsals, it was wonderful to see the room full of almost 50 writers (from both productions) and to hear such a varied range of opinions and insights expressed through the plays. I am very grateful to everyone who has made it possible by sharing their work with us.

Jim Culleton

Credits | Tiny Plays For Ireland

Tiny Plays for Ireland were first produced by Fishamble: The New Play Company on 15 March 2012 at the Project Arts Centre, Dublin with the following cast and production team:

Man 1	**Peter Daly**
Man 2	**Don Wycherly**
Man 3	**Steve Blount**
Woman 1	**Mary Murray**
Woman 2	**Kate Stanley Brennan**
Boy	**Robert Donnelly**
Voice over in *A Body*	**Sean Doupe**
Director	**Jim Culleton**
Dramaturgy	**Gavin Kostick**
Set Designer	**Sabine Dargent**
Costume Designer	**Niamh Lunny**
Lighting Designer	**Paul Keogan**

Sound Designers	**Ivan Birthistle and Vincent Doherty**
Producer	**Marketa Dowling**
PR	**Sinead O'Doherty at Gerry Lundberg PR**
Production Manager	**Des Kenny**
Stage Director	**Diarmuid O'Quigley**
Stage Manager	**Clare Howe**
Hair & Make-Up	**Val Sherlock**
Graphic Designer	**Dave Darcy**
Stills	**Pat Redmond**
Polish Accent Coach	**Anna Wolf**
Chaperone	**Emma Ryan**
Assistant Director	**Aisling Smith**
Costume Assistant	**Tullia Giacomelli**

Running Order | Tiny Plays For Ireland 1

A Life by Ronan Geoghegan

The Nation's Assets by Michelle Read

Tuesday Evening (Following the News) by Darren Donohue

The Audition by Rory Nolan

Guaranteed Irish by Colin Murphy

It's a Lovely Day, Bill Withers by Jody O'Neill

Sure This Is It by Ciara Ni Chuirc

Unrequited by Michael Cussen

Where Will We Go by Dermot Bolger

Safety Announcement

By Joseph O'Connor

*An **Usher** in tuxedo walks onto the playing area.*

Usher: Welcome to Project Arts Centre and FISHAMBLE'S production TINY PLAYS FOR IRELAND.

Please take note of your nearest fire exit, which may be behind you, and ensure that your mobile phone is switched completely off and not left on silent.

Photography and filming of any type is strictly prohibited in the auditorium.

Please note that patrons who leave the performance will not be readmitted.

You can find more information on our programme and to book tickets online at www.projectartscentre.ie

Please enjoy the show

Fáilte chuig Ionad Ealaíon Project

Tabhair faoi deara an doras éalaithe is giorra duit, b'fhéidir go bhfuil sé taobh thiar duit agus déan cinnte go bhfuil do ghuthán póca ní amháin curtha ina dtost ach múctha amach is amach.

Tá cosc iomlán ar ghriangrafadóireacht le splanc taobh istigh den amharclann…

(He now becomes aware that a man in the audience has his hand up for some moments.)

Audience Member: Excuse me?

Usher: *(nonplussed)* Yes?

Audience Member: Mr Daly?

Usher: Yes.

Audience Member: Mr Peter Daly of Le Fanu Avenue?

Usher: Who are you?

Audience Member: I'm sorry to interrupt, but can I have a word? When you're ready?

Usher: Look, I'm actually trying to work here. What do you think you're doing?

Audience Member: I'm a court-appointed officer and I'm here to serve you with a summons for mortgage arrears.

Usher: For God's sake, this is a public place. A play is about to start!

Audience Member/Bailiff: You've been avoiding me for weeks. You haven't returned my calls. I called up to you at the house and you pretended you were out.

Usher: I didn't.

Audience Member/Bailiff: I saw you through the curtains.

Usher: I don't *have* curtains.

Bailiff: Don't be fuckin' smart, pal. I meant the venetian blinds. *[He approaches.]* I'm authorised to repossess goods from you to the value of five thousand euros. That's the way it's gonna be, pal. It's payback time.

Usher: I don't have it, I swear. What are you suggesting?

Bailiff: I'm suggesting you pay me. I'll give you five minutes.

Usher: Be reasonable, for God's sake. Can we talk about this after the show?

Bailiff: The time for talking's over. I need the money now.

*(The **Usher** thinks for a moment.)*

Usher: Can anyone in the audience loan me five thousand euros?

(Silence.)

Usher: A tenner?

Bailiff: Of course they can't lend you five grand! Look at the state of them! They're broke! You don't think they'd be dressed like alcoholic tramps otherwise??

Usher: I don't have it. I swear. What you want me to do?

Bailiff: Right so. I'm performing a citizen's arrest on you.

*(In different parts of the audience, two **Heavies** stand up. They approach the stage menacingly.)*

Usher *(backing away fearfully)* **LADS!**

(From backstage, every member of the cast very quickly appears, some costumed, some in wigs, some in their own clothes. Many of them quickly produce improvised weapons: coshes, chair legs, lengths of chain, bricks. An actor dressed as Hamlet produces a chainsaw.)

Bailiff: Do you think that pack of gobshites scares me? The money! Or else!

Usher: I warn you. These are trained actors. You don't want to mess around.

*(One of the **Actors** mimes producing a shotgun. He locks and loads.)*

Bailiff: (*to the actor*) What in the name of Jaysus do you think you're doing?

Usher: The arts have power. Don't fuck with them, I warn you. They *voted for Michael D Higgins!*

Bailiff: Right so. I'm sick of this.

*(As **Heavy One** approaches, the **Actor** BLASTS him with the mimed shotgun. The **Heavy** falls to the ground, writhing in agony. The **Actor** turns his invisible shotgun on the second **Heavy** and BLASTS him too. The **Heavy** collapses. The **Actor** ruthlessly reloads and finishes him off on the ground. A gang of other **Actors** then mime producing flick knives and attack the **Bailiff** with them, knifing him until he collapses in appalling and overacted agony.)*

(All three bodies are dragged off stage by the company.)

Usher: Ladies and gentlemen, please excuse that interruption. Turn your phones off ... Or else.

Poster Boy

By Antonia Hart

*Platform at Pearse Station, Dublin **Mum** and young teenage son
Seán are sitting on a bench waiting for a DART, she's upright
and alert, he's lolling on the bench with his legs sticking out, one
of them bouncing in time to the music he's listening to on his iPod.
Mum is dressed in trendy mum clothes – an Avoca-style tunic,
faux fur-lined gilet, leggings, skinny boots, with a slouchy, soft
leather handbag. Good haircut and makeup. **Seán** wears school
uniform – grey trousers with tie poking out of pocket, white open-
necked shirt, navy jumper.*

*Something catches **Mum's** eye. The audience can't see it.*

Mum: *(nudging son)* I can't believe they've done it again.

Seán: Hmm?

*(**Mum** pulls his earphone out of the ear nearest to her.)*

Seán: *(sitting up)* Mum! Get off! What?

*(**Seán** snatches back earphone.)*

Mum: *(gestures)* Did you see the poster?

Seán: *(rolls eyes)* That crisp one?

Mum: Yes, can you believe they've done it again?

Seán: *(puts earphone back in)* I quite like it.

Mum: *(pulls earphone out again)* You what?

Seán: *(stuffs earphones in pocket, shrugs)* It's OK.

Mum: How is it OK?

Seán: I like it. It doesn't make me buy the crisps or not buy the crisps. It's just a picture. Lighten up.

Mum: But Seán, do you think it's right to use images of women in that way?

Seán: I dunno.

Mum: *(exasperated)* But we've talked about this!

Seán: *You've* talked about it.

Mum: Well, anyway, I've said it's wrong.

Seán: They didn't make the models do it, did they? They wanted to, they got paid, what's the problem?

Mum: The problem is it's perpetuating the idea that women are nothing more than sexual objects.

Seán: *(pulls out earphones again and inspects them; picks something off one of them)* I dunno what perpetuating is.

Mum: Keeping it going.

Seán: OK but if it's women doing it that's OK. Why should you tell other women how to be?

Mum: I don't want to tell anyone how to be! The whole point of the struggle for equal rights was that women would have choices. I'm not saying the models shouldn't work as models or shouldn't show their bodies. Of course they, as women, should have a choice.

Seán: Well I don't get it then.

Mum: Well, I suppose it's the advertising agency I have a problem with, and the crisp company themselves. They are the ones who are promoting the idea that a woman's place in society is determined by how attractive she is, by how big her…

Seán: Breasts?

Mum: Well, yes, by how big her breasts are. Or by how … (*whispers*) *sexually available* … she is.

Seán: Nobody cares, Mum.

Mum: How can you say that?

Seán: Nobody cares. If one of my mates sees that poster he doesn't go, "Oh OK, women should definitely earn less than men" or "Oh right, like women should do more washing up or whatever." If you see the poster you just go, "That's a fit girl." If you like the crisps you buy them. If you don't, you don't. You don't have to go jumping around about it.

Mum: I'm not jumping around.

Seán: OK, well you don't have to keep educating me.

Mum: It's my job.

Seán: (*sighs*) I know, Mum. What I *mean* is that you don't have to keep rabbitting on about *this* one. I don't have a crap idea about women or anything and I know perfectly well what the poster is saying. But because I know it it doesn't affect me. I'm not thick, you know.

Mum: You can't be sure it doesn't affect you.

Seán: I can. Here's the train.

*(**Seán** gets earphones out of pocket, sticks them in ears, turns up volume on iPod. Sound of distant train rumbling.)*

Mum: *(raises voice)* I just want you to have a good level of awareness. What music are you listening to?

Seán: *(removes one earphone)* What?

Mum: What music are you listening to?

Seán: That Eminem and Rihanna song.

(Rumbling of train gets louder.)

Mum: That one that says if she tries to leave he's going to tie her to the bed?

Seán: It's just music, Mum.

*(**Seán** puts earphone back in and walks off.)*

Mum: So it is that one? I assume you've looked up those lyrics on the web. Seán! Do you know what misogyny means? Can you hear me?

White Food

By Ardal O'Hanlon

The scene is the lounge of a well-run hotel in a border town on a Sunday morning.

Offstage, a Sunday morning crooner sings 'Ode to Billie Joe' while playing his plinky keyboard.

Frank (30), a native with metropolitan flourishes, sits hung over on a banquette. There is an overnight bag on the floor beside him and an unfinished pint on the table. He is joined by his brother Seamus (33), dressed as a referee, two fresh pints in his hands.

Seamus: That was some night. *(Drinks)*

Frank: Oh.

Seamus: Ha?

Frank: Oh-hoh.

Seamus: Wasn't it though?

Frank: Yeah.

Seamus: A deadly night. Am I right?

Frank: I should be off, Seamus.

Seamus: Did you see Mammy's face?

Frank: I did.

Seamus: Ha?

Frank: Oh now.

Seamus: Ha? Do you know what your problem is?

Frank: No.

Seamus: You're aloof. *(Drinks)* Did you know that?

Frank: *(drinks)*

Seamus: No offence, Frank. You don't join in. *(He suddenly bursts into song along with the offstage crooner.)* "… from Choctaw ridge, today Billie Joe McAllister jumped off the Tallahatchie Bridge." *(Abruptly)* You have no sense of … community. *(Beat)* Some spread!

Frank: Yeah …

Seamus: A credit to all concerned. Ha? *(Drinks)*

Frank: Well …

Seamus: Well what?

Frank: It was a bit …

Seamus: A bit what?

Frank: A bit … you know …

Seamus: Ha?

Frank: Gloopy! The food. A bit on the gloopy side.

Seamus: What are you on about? Frank? Gloopy? Ha? What the fuck are you on about? It was deadly. That's what it was.

Frank: Sorry.

Seamus: Make no mistake about that, whatsoever. A deadly spread. Is what it was. *(Drinks)*

Frank: It's just.

Seamus: Ha? *(Looks at his watch.)*

Frank: It was all … white.

Seamus: It was a buffet, Frank.

Frank: The potato salad was white.

Seamus: So what?

Frank: The coleslaw? What colour was that?

Seamus: White. Of course. Fair play to it.

Frank: The apple and celery? The coronation chicken?

Seamus: Stop. Stop.

Frank: All white.

Seamus: You're whetting me appetite. I'm salivating.

Frank: Why? *(Drinks)*

Seamus: It went down well. That's the main thing.

Frank: Even the ham was white.

Seamus: *(stands up, angry)* That was turkey. In fairness, Frank. That was fucking turkey, *(slams table)* so it was. No need to be so contrary. So up your own hole. So aloof. Your whole fucking life. *(Sits down again)*

Frank: I'm sorry.

Seamus: It was Mammy's birthday.

Frank: Exactly.

Seamus: Her eightieth fucking birthday. Did you see her fucking face? Did you? It wouldn't matter if the food was blue. The important thing is everyone was there. Including, as we all know, you. The apple, and celery, of her fucking eye. *(Drinks)*

Frank: I'm not saying.

Seamus: *(sits)* Some crowd all the same. Ha?

Frank: It was.

Seamus: Wasn't it? Were you talking to Hawkeye?

Frank: I was.

Seamus: And Bullets?

Frank: Yeah.

Seamus: And Travis?

Frank: Just to say hello.

Seamus: "Well boys. What's cooking?" Travis! Ha? "What's cooking?" *(Beat)* And the Flynn girl? *(Looks at him meaningfully)*

Frank: *(drinks)*

Seamus: Yeah. Ha? I never seen you so animated. The pair of yous.

Frank: Well.

Seamus: You missed the cutting of the cake anyway.

Frank: Did I?

Seamus: Mammy's cake. Mammy's big fucking white cake.

Frank: We went out for a smoke. *(Drinks)*

Seamus: All I'm saying is.

Frank: Sure.

Seamus: Right? That's all I'm saying. (*He stands up, drains pint.*) Great to see you, Frank. (***Frank** stands, they hug.*)

Frank: You too, Seamus.

Seamus: Last time I reffed a match in Tydavnet, I sent five men off, the match was abandoned, and I was locked in the boot of a car for over two hours.

Frank: (*laughs*)

Seamus: (*serious*) No laughing matter, Frank. The Clontibret centre half back is in a coma ever since.

Frank: Jesus.

Seamus: Above in Drogheda. So he is. Drooling. Surrounded by friends and family.

Frank: Ha?

Seamus: And a fiddler from Dromiskin who comes of a Sunday to play a few jigs and reels by the bed. She's a married woman.

Frank: For fuck's sake, Seamus.

Seamus: With two children.

Frank: Jesus Christ.

Seamus: That's all I'm saying. (*Suddenly bursts into song again*) "… and she and Billie Joe were throwing something off the Tallahatchie Bridge …"

(***Seamus** goes off singing 'Ode to Billie Joe.' **Frank** stays put. Takes a very long drink. Lights out.)*

Beat Him Like A Badger

By Rosaleen McDonagh
translated by Agnieszka Nowak

Two teenage girls sitting on a bench in the corridor in front of the principal's office. They don't talk to each other. The monologues are criss-crossed, as if they are not aware of each other's presence. **Jessica Ward**, *Traveller, and* **Aga Nowak,** *Polish, two teenagers.*

Jessica: Daddy put suit on. I have to wait in the corridor while he talks to the principal of the school. He kept saying to me, "Things are bad enough for us in this town without you making it worse. We don't have the money for that window if that school comes looking for it."

Aga: *Najlepsze przyjaciółki, Irlandzka Cyganka i Polka. Siedzę tutaj, bo kocham Jessikę Ward.* Best friends, the Traveller beoir and Polish dziewczuna. I'm sitting here because I love Jessica Ward. Living in the town for the last seven years, going to the same shops, chapel, doctor – and the same school. She won't listen when I try to say sorry. Jessica Ward, I hurt her.

Jessica: Aga Nowak, my sisters said, Polish people will soon learn from the settled young ones how to hate Travellers.

She was my friend. I trusted her. In the site older beoirs saying no Pavee fein would marry me in a school uniform.

Aga: The feelings were so strong about Travellers in this town, like back home. Polish people hate the Roma community. My father had seen the news and said, "*Jak I Romscy Cyganie to klamcy I zlodzieje.* Travellers and Roma people; they're all liars and thieves."

Jessica: Remembering all the fun we had. "Are you related?" the girls were all asking. The *X-Factor* winner, Shane Ward. They think all Pavees are cousins so I wrote, "Love from Shane". It was our joke on all the girls in our year. It didn't matter that he was a Traveller.

Aga: Over the years, she'd explain about Travellers. But I knew it was the same to how we treated the Roma at home in Poland. That morning, on the twenty-second of December, the day after the verdict, at school, I didn't want to be near Jessica Ward.

Jessica: The Joyces saying, "Well, what was that Pavee fein doing there in the first place? He was up to no good." The O'Connor beoirs said, "A settled fein killed one of us and got away with it." One of the McDonagh young ones said, "A verdict from an all-settled jury. What do you expect?"

Aga: They asked me about being Polish. "Did we have Travellers in Poland?" I was ashamed to tell them about how we treated Roma people back home in my town.

Jessica: They think we're all the same. And now I think buffers are all the same. She won't be expelled. Saying "sorry," that's no good to me now. As far as I'm concerned Aga Nowak is just another buffer bitch in this school. Me begging a Polish buffer to be my friend. Fuck the lot of you, "Dirty, filthy, buffers."

Aga: They were shouting at her. "Why don't you fuck off back to that knacker site where you belong? Ye can't be educated, you're animals! Frightening old people."

Jessica: My Pavee rage was building up inside me. The stone was big and heavy. I flung it straight through the window of the school.

Aga: The rain was running down my face. Tears stinging my eyes. Calling Jessica's name but it was lost in the December wind. A newspaper swirled around the yard. I put my foot on it – The headlines read, "Beat him like a badger."

The King's Shilling C.1808

By Mark Hennessy

Recruiting Sergeant: There ye go lad. (*slapping down tankard of ale onto tavern table*) Now, get that down ye an' tell old Bill one more time. What's to be 'ad livin' out yer life in this godforsaken place, eh lad? Eh?

Local Yokel: Well Sergeant, sure hasn't me family been livin' here for, for . . . .

Recruiting Sergeant: For what lad, for what?

Local Yokel: For such a long time, Sergeant, such a long time! Why would I ever want to leave? Sure isn't it beautiful here?

Recruiting Sergeant: (*looking around*) Aye, that it is lad, that it is. Godforsaken mind, but beautiful all the same.

Local Yokel: (*nodding sagely*)

Recruiting Sergeant: But don't ye wish for adventure lad, eh? Away from the sheep an' the pigs an' the cows, eh? Real adventure – an' what could be more adventurous than this, eh? (*pointing to regimental drummer in full dress uniform with scarlet coat*) Take the King's shilling lad, an' join up! Take the shilling an' march off to foreign parts to do battle wiv the nefarious French an' that damned Corsican, Bonaparte! Would ye stand back lad, an' watch the Frogs gobble up all of Europe, an' Ireland too? Well, would ye? An' all the while knowin' ye could've done something to 'elp King an' country?

Local Yokel: But Sergeant, *(frowning)* me da says that any enemy of the English is a true friend of Ireland!

Recruiting Sergeant: Saints above, lad! Now, I've no wish to be contradictin' yer dear old da's word, but the man's never been a mile from a cowshite, 'as he? An' what could he be knowin' of those blackguards, the French, an' their plans for dominion, eh, if he ain't ever even seen one?

Local Yokel: Well, seein' as ye put it like that Sergeant . . .

Recruiting Sergeant: I do lad, I do. The Frenchies ain't to be trusted, see? Why, I remember the battle of Talavera, 'avin just put a lead ball into one of 'em. He says, *(affecting French accent)* "Please, please, no more! I surrender, I am hurt! Please, no more!" And so I makes to 'elp the poor bugger an' ye know what 'appens then, lad, eh? The little bastard slips out a pistol an' points it at old Bill! Well, I'm 'avin none of it, so I takes me musket and I gives 'im 12 inches of Sheffield steel, so I do, an' gut that Frenchie like a fish! *(wide-eyed and miming action dramatically)* Guts 'im I do! An' sure enough, don't the Frog fall down dead as a doornail, stainin' me good honest soldier's boots wiv 'is traitorous Frog blood!

Local Yokel: *(wide-eyed, open-mouthed)* Really, Sergeant??!

Recruiting Sergeant: Upon the Lord's prayer, lad, that's 'ow it was. So, do ye see, lad, 'ow duplicitous these Frenchies are, eh? Why would a man trust 'em wiv anything of worth, eh? A gun, a woman, or even a few bob! Why lad, when calm seas turn rough, they'll turn on ye, mark my word.

Local Yokel: Well, Sergeant . . .

Recruiting Sergeant: Enlist lad, enlist! Take the King's coat and 'is shilling too! Now, *there's* a currency you can be relyin' on!

Local Yokel: Oooh, I'm not so sure now . . .

Recruiting Sergeant: *(gesturing to serving girl)* Another tankard lass, an' be quick! Old Bill ain't filled 'is regimental quota yet . . . !

Between Us We Have Everything

By Karl O'Neill

An empty space. Brighter light off SL than SR.

*An **Old Man** walks slowly on from SL. A **Young Boy** runs on from SR.*

They meet centre stage.

Boy: Hello!

Man: Hello.

Boy: Who are you?

Man: Oh, just ... an old man. On my travels.

Boy: Where do you come from?

Man: *(indicates)* Back there.

Boy: Where are you going?

Man: *(indicates)* This way.

Boy: That's where I'm from.

Man: Yes.

Boy: *(indicates)* And that's where I'm going. At least, I think so.

Man: I'm sure that is the way. *(The **Boy** seems reluctant.)*

Boy: Is it a long way?

Man: It may seem so to you. But it isn't really.

Boy: What's it like?

Man: The journey?

Boy: *(points)* That way.

Man: It's ... hard to say.

Boy: There's an awful lot of it.

Man: There is, and yet ... it doesn't seem so long, not from here, not from where I am.

Boy: *(pointing back)* I've come all that way.

Man: Yes, I can see that. It's not very far, you know. Not from where I am.

(Pause.)

Boy: Would you like to sit down?

Man: I'd like to, but ...

Boy: But what?

Man: At my age, I'm afraid if I sit down I might never get up again.

Boy: *(accepts this)* Okay.

Man: Does the way ahead scare you?

Boy: A little.

Man: That's understandable. But there's no need, you know. To be afraid.

Boy: Is it dangerous?

Man: No. Not if you watch where you're going. It's actually quite exciting.

Boy: Then why did you leave?

Man: Well, I haven't really left. I'm just going on, continuing my journey. This way can be quite exciting too.

Boy: *(unsure)* You think?

Man: I hope.

(Pause. They pass each other, carefully.)

Boy: Will you be coming back this way?

Man: No. I don't think so.

Boy: Will we ever meet again?

Man: It's unlikely.

(Pause.)

Boy: *(looks SR)* I'm scared.

Man: *(looks SL)* So am I.

(They turn to look at each other, and laugh.)

Boy: It's silly to be scared, isn't it?

Man: *(nods)* You know, between us we have everything ... What I have lived, you have left to live; and what you have lived is left to me.

Boy: I haven't lived very long.

Man: No, but you are living the most precious time. The best time.

Boy: You don't have much time left.

Man: True. I must go. Make the most of it.

Boy: Goodbye then.

Man: Goodbye. Enjoy! *(The **Boy** runs off SR.)* You shouldn't run. *(Looks SL)* If you knew what was ahead of you, you would walk so slowly, *(walking off)* ever so slowly … ever so slowly …

(Fade lights to sunset. Black.)

Don't Take It Personally

By Rachel Fehily

Two barristers walk on stage from left and right, a man and a woman, wearing wigs and gowns, laden with briefs and texting on their mobile phones. They look at each other at the same time from a distance. Man jerks his head to the woman. She beckons him. They sidle up to each other in the middle of the stage outside a courtroom door, which has two steps leading up to it. On it hangs a crooked 'in camera' sign. They put their briefs and phones down on the steps.

Mark: *(pointing a finger)* You're drinking like a fish.

Judy: *(throwing both hands up in the air)* And you're a lazy bitch.

Mark: *(folding arms in front of body)* You haven't paid this month's maintenance.

Judy: *(folding arms as well in a defensive gesture)* My business is going down the toilet. I'm living in a bedsit. Why should I pay for your botox and brazillians?

Mark: *(holding up her hand in his face)* Talk to the hand. We're in the list next week. I'll let you whinge to the judge.

Judy: *(turning away)* You're expecting the order for four grand a month to continue? Have you seen the discovery? Why don't you go out and get a job you lazy bitch?

Mark: I've three children under twelve and haven't worked since 1999. How am I supposed to find a job in this recession?

Judy: You'd no problem leaving the kids with the au pairs and spending all day in the gym when we were living together.

Mark: Why don't we let the judge decide? He's not going to be impressed by your behaviour.

Judy: Go ahead. At the end of the day it's division of the assets. Shagging my secretary isn't a crime.

Mark: Doesn't make you look good.

Judy: It's not a beauty contest.

Mark: Lucky for you. *(Laughing)* I saw your fat, red face earlier.

Judy: *(laughing as well)* You're no looker either, despite all the treatments. If we can't agree I suppose the house will have to be sold.

Mark: *(whining)* I want to stay in the house. I can't move far away from the school and all the kids' friends.

Judy: Well you can't afford to buy me out.

Mark: I'm only looking for a right of residency until the kids finish school.

Judy: *(suddenly friendly)* … then a sale? Fifty-fifty split?

Mark: *(putting his arm around her shoulder)* Maybe, if you can do something about the maintenance.

Judy: If you're prepared to be realistic.

Mark: (*staring into **Judy's** eyes*) There might be no need for a forensic accountant to look at your business, and I wouldn't have to report you to the taxman for all those cash transactions.

Judy: (*holding **Mark** tightly*) I would rather you were at home minding the children but I can't afford the four grand a month.

Mark: (*snuggling into **Judy's** chest*) I could live on a bit less, get part-time work, but I need you to be reasonable.

Judy: I'm the most reasonable man you ever married (*puffing out her chest*)

Mark: You're the only man I ever married. (*looking coy*)

(*Both barristers look at each other and pull away suddenly.*)

Judy: (*suddenly businesslike*) Okay, I need to go and talk to my client.

Mark: (*similar tone*) And I'm sure I can talk mine into doing a deal on the maintenance.

Judy: No need for the stress of a full hearing.

Mark: Who wants that?

(*They bow to each other and pick up their briefs.*)

Judy: In or out tonight sweetie?

Mark: Oh let's stay in darling, I'm shattered. Why don't we pick up a Mexican from Baggot Street?

Judy: Perfect.

(*They kiss each other passionately and walk off stage together.*)

Pastoral Care

By Gerald Murphy

Fade up lights.

A career guidance teacher's office in a second-level school. A small, cramped space overwhelmed by books, pamphlets, filing systems, posters.

*Sitting behind a desk is **Ms Flynn** (50s). She wears spectacles on a cord around her neck. **Mr Gormley** (40s) is standing to the side of **Emer** (12). He has a copybook in his hand. **Ms Flynn** and **Mr Gormley** are dressed in aged, faded clothing. **Emer** wears a tidy school uniform.*

***Ms Flynn** is smiling at **Emer**. **Emer** is not sure why she has been brought here. She never gets into trouble.*

Emer: *(to **Ms Flynn**, in response to a question, uncertain)* … Is it when someone steals something? … Like the thoughts or writing of someone else and they pretend that it's their own?

Flynn: … That's exactly what it is!

Gormley: *(still not entirely convinced)* … Can you spell it?

Emer: … Em … p – l – a – g – i – a – r – i – s – m.

Flynn: Wonderful!

Gormley: … You're new to the area – aren't you?

Emer: *(uncertain)* … Yeah.

Flynn: And how are you finding it?

Emer: *(uncertain)* … All right.

Gormley: *(presenting the copybook and quoting from it)* This is a terrific essay.

"Freedom of opinion and expression, tolerance, understanding, the right to an education" – you're just at a whole other level.

Emer: *(Is that good or bad?)* … Oh. Thanks?

Gormley: *(while walking over to the door)* … But it's just …

*(**Mr Gormley** opens the door. SFX: The roar of noisy corridors)*

Gormley: *(with door open)* … They'll eat you alive.

*(**Mr Gormley** closes the door. SFX: The roar ceasing)*

Flynn: *(to **Emer**)* … We thought you might benefit from some words of advice, Emer.

Gormley: *(returning to the desk)* … What's your name?

Emer: *(again uncertain, seeing as they already know her name)* … em … Emer Mc Evoy?

Flynn: If a teacher asks your name – just say "What?"

Emer: *(doesn't respond)*

Flynn: "What?"

Emer: … What?

Flynn: … A little more impertinence.

Emer: *(tries being impertinent)* … What?

Gormley: … Not bad.

Flynn: If a teacher asks you to perform a task in class – don't do it straight away –

Gormley: or just pretend you can't do it –

Flynn: – or complain and say something like, "It's stupid!"

*(**Emer** doesn't respond.)*

Gormley: … Go on.

Emer: … It's stupid.

Gormley: *(with an accent)* "Stupid!"

Emer: *(tries the accent)* … Stupid.

Gormley: Yeah better – good!

Flynn: … Make sure you get caught using your phone in class –

Gormley: And if the teacher says "Are you texting?"

Flynn: Just say, "No I'm on Facebook."

Emer: *(not sure if she has to repeat this)* … No …

*(Mr Gormley is encouraging **Emer** to continue.)*

Emer: … I'm on Facebook.

Gormley: That's it.

Flynn: Otherwise only speak when you're spoken to.

Gormley: And for God's sake don't use big words.

Flynn: … And don't forget to work on your accent.

*(Both teachers smile at **Emer**. She smiles back uncertainly.)*

Gormley: *(continuing to smile)* … You'll get there – don't worry.

*(The smiling continues. **Emer** widens her smile.)*

Gormley: … They call me 'Bottleneck' by the way.

Flynn: … And I'm 'Cow', just 'Cow.'

Gormley: *(to **Flynn**, correcting her)* 'Moo face.'

Flynn: *(to **Gormley**)* 'Moo face?'

Gormley: Apparently.

Flynn: *(half to herself)* Same theme – new twist.

Gormley: *(to **Emer**)* Mr Peters is 'Paedo'. Ms O'Connell is 'Crabs'. You'll pick up the rest.

Flynn: … We're delighted to have you here, Emer, but sometimes being smart is – knowing when to play dumb. It's a bit of a life lesson actually.

(The smiles return.)

Gormley: … So we want you to produce terrible work from now on – appalling spelling, grammar; zero punctuation; awful handwriting –

Flynn: – as well as good work.

Gormley: Two copies of everything.

Flynn: … All the other teachers will be informed, but your classmates will think you're just as bad as them.

Gormley: … Okay?

Emer: *(uncertain)* … Okay.

Flynn: … Have you any questions for us?

Emer: … Em … no I don't think so.

Flynn: … Great! If you think of anything don't be afraid to knock – all right?

*(**Emer's** half smile)*

Gormley: And if any of them see you coming out of here just tell them we were giving you an official warning.

Flynn: All right?

*(**Emer** nods.)*

Gormley: Well done.

*(**Mr Gormley** makes a gesture indicating it's time for **Emer** to leave.*

***Emer** gets up off the chair and **Mr Gormley** accompanies her to the door and opens it for her. SFX: We hear the corridor roar again.*

***Emer** exits.*

***Mr Gormley** closes the door, staying in the room. SFX: roar ceasing)*

Gormley: What do you think?

Flynn: … I think … this time … we could win.

Mr Gormley: *(smiles, opens the door onto the roaring corridor and exits. SFX as above)*

Ms Flynn: *(smiles)*

(LFX: Fade lights down.)

Broken

By Deirdre Kinahan

Tom is standing outside a building that houses a small, private primary school. There is a flower box full of daffodils with homemade bees and butterflies standing on sticks in the soil.

Shane: Howaya Tom.

Tom: Shane!

Shane: Yes.

Tom: Good to see you … good to see you. I was just passing.

Shane: Ahhh right.

Tom: And the daffodils, well! … The daffodils caught my eye.

Shane: O yes, they brighten up the place.

Tom: They do … and I wondered did the children plant them? Did the children plant them?

Shane: They did I think. Yes, they did actually, Tom.

Tom: Senior Infants was it?

Shane: Well … em … I'm not sure…

Tom: Oh I just thought it might be Senior Infants? Tania's class.

Shane: Maybe…

Tom: Because she loves planting.

Shane: Does she?

Tom: Yes, anything … she loved … I mean she loves anything … any time in the garden …

Shane: Ahh yes. Good.

Tom: Yes.

(Pause.)

Shane: So how are you doing, Tom?

Tom: I'm doing well thanks, Shane. I was in work today actually.

Shane: Were you?

Tom: Some consulting.

Shane: Oh excellent.

Tom: IFSC.

Shane: Excellent.

Tom: It's a small firm … they installed a new finance package … so I think the whole team will need retraining.

Shane: Well!

Tom: Yes. Should keep me spinning for a few weeks.

Shane: Excellent.

Tom: Yeah.

(Pause.)

Tom: So I happened to be passing ....

Shane: Right.

Tom: And it's almost three.

Shane: It is.

Tom: So I thought ... they'll be out soon. Tania will be out soon.

Shane: She will.

Tom: Because I like to see her most days ... if I can, Shane.

Shane: Of course you do.

Tom: She's growing up fast.

Shane: She is. They all do.

Tom: And Tadhgh ... starting in September!

Shane: Yes, we're looking forward to him.

Tom: "The head of me" ... they say.

Shane: Is that right?

Tom: "Spit"!

Shane: Gas!

Tom: Yes.

(Pause.)

Tom: So I thought I'd just hold on ... till three.

Shane: And does Tania know you'll be here, Tom, or Marie?

Tom: Marie? No. Why would Marie know?

Shane: Because we have to get permission. I know you know that, Tom. We have to get permission from Marie.

Tom: I'm just … I was just. I was passing and … I want to see my daughter, Shane.

Shane: Of course. And I can understand that. But I'm afraid I can't have another incident, Tom.

Tom: There won't be another incident. Jesus Christ, I'm entitled to see my own children.

Shane: I know you are, Tom. But there's an order. Now you know that there's an order so its not fair for you to do this … to the school, Tom, … or to Tania.

Tom: Oh… I see. I see, Shane. She has you now too. Marie has you now too. She has you all fucking poisoned.

Shane: I really think you should move on now, Tom.

Tom: Well I'm not fucking moving on. I want to see my daughter.

Shane: But you're frightening her.

Tom: I'm frightening her?

Shane: And I don't honestly believe you want to do that.

Tom: I'm frightening her?

Shane: With all this.

Tom: With all what?

Shane: You can't keep coming here.

Tom: I enrolled her here. I'm her father.

Shane: I know that. We all know that. But there are procedures … and you can't take Tania without permission, Marie's permission, Tom. You know that … And you knew that … there are consequences…

Tom: I'm entitled to see her. I want to see her.

Shane: Don't make me call the guards, Tom.

Tom: Have you any idea? Any idea, Shane? What this is like. *(pause)* I'm not a fucking monster.

Shane: No. You're not a monster, Tom. But we all have to play by the rules. And we have to think about Tania.

Tom: Tania is all I think about. And Tadhgh.

Shane: So you see … it's best then, to move on.

(Pause.)

Shane: Isn't it?

(Pause.)

Shane: Is that okay, Tom?

Shane: Okay?

Tom: Okay.

Shane: Good man.

*(**Tom** turns to leave. **Tom** turns back.)*

Tom: But you'll tell her I was here?

*(**Shane** doesn't respond.)*

Tom: You'll tell her I saw the flowers?

Shane: I think it's best not to, Tom. Don't you?

*(**Tom** stands eye to eye with **Shane**.*

*Then **Tom** turns.*

***Tom** leaves.*

***Shane** remains watching till **Tom** is gone.)*

Rainout

By Jesse Weaver

Catriona's apartment. It's raining outside.

Lilly, American, dressed in a full softball uniform, green, a huge shamrock on the front. A softball glove in her hands. She's drenched, shivering.

Catriona, Irish, dressed in pink pyjamas.

Lilly: 'Kay.

Catriona: Okay.

(Pause. Rain.)

Catriona: They cancelled your softball thing?

Lilly: Yeah. It's a rainout.

Catriona: A rainout?

Lilly: Cuz it got rained out.

Catriona: That's too bad.

Lilly: Sucks. The third this month. Freakin' Ireland. The one thing I miss ...

Catriona: Yeah?

Lilly: One thing I miss about home ...

Catriona: I know.

*(**Lilly** shakes her head.)*

Lilly: ... sucks ...

(Pause.)

Lilly: *(cont.)* Can I use your shower?

Catriona: No. I don't think –

Lilly: I'm freezing.

Catriona: I don't think that's a good idea.

Lilly: Can I borrow some of your clothes?

Catriona: You should probably go, don't you think?

Lilly: Why? Just cuz –

Catriona: It's awkward.

Lilly: Just cuz you said, just cuz we broke up –

Catriona: We broke up two minutes ago.

Lilly: Yeah, but me wanting a shower doesn't have anything to do with that.

Catriona: Use your own shower.

Lilly: It's in Ballsbridge.

Catriona: Get a taxi.

Lilly: I don't have my wallet.

Catriona: Get a bus.

Lilly: Look. Look.

Catriona: What?

Lilly: Look, I don't appreciate this. Have the courtesy –

Catriona: Appreciate ...?

Lilly: Have the courtesy to tell me to just fuck off –

Catriona: Fuck off.

Lilly: Instead of. Instead of. This passive aggressive. This Irish. This passive aggressive Irish shit. This tea and then a biscuit and goodbye now. This meek, this crass, this crassly meek fucking nonsense shit.

Catriona: I'm pregnant.

(Pause.)

Lilly: If that don't beat the band.

Catriona: If ... what?

Lilly: What?

Catriona: Who else ...?

Lilly: What?

Catriona: Who in the world says that?

Lilly: Says what?

Catriona: "Beat the band."

Lilly: Can't be.

Catriona: What?

Lilly: You can't be. How could you be?

(Pause.)

Lilly: *(cont.)* While we were ...?

Catriona: Once off.

Lilly: Once ...?

Catriona: A once off.

Lilly: While we were ...?

Catriona: Yeah.

Lilly: 'Kay...

Catriona: Okay ...

(Pause.)

Lilly: That's why.

Catriona: What's why?

Lilly: Did you think ...?

Catriona: What's why?

Lilly: Did you think I'd tell you to fuck off. Just cuz you're – ?

Catriona: No.

Lilly: Cuz I wouldn't have.

Catriona: Look –

Lilly: No, this is. I'm. This is. When you think about this –

Catriona: No –

Lilly: Wait, when you think about this. I've been waiting. I've been waiting. For when this place felt like home?

Catriona: Jesus.

Lilly: And this could be the start of –

Catriona: No.

Lilly: A family. No what?

Catriona: Got a flight booked.

Lilly: A...? A what?

Catriona: Flight booked. I'm not doin' it.

Lilly: You're ...?

Catriona: I'm not havin' it.

Lilly: Can we talk about it?

Catriona: Talk ...?

Lilly: Can we at least talk about – ?

Catriona: What the fuck business is it of yours?

Lilly: What business ...?

Catriona: Did *you* get me pregnant? Is this your baby?

Lilly: What kind of – ?

Catriona: Because if you did, let me know.

Lilly: Who was it?

Catriona: Due a Nobel Prize, then.

Lilly: WHO WAS IT?

Catriona: No one. No one you know. A once off.

(Pause.)

Lilly: Two years. Me and you.

Catriona: Yeah.

Lilly: Two years.

Catriona: Hasn't been right for a while. Hasn't felt right for a while.

Lilly: No. But. No.

Catriona: 'Kay ...?

*(**Lilly** nods.)*

Lilly: Okay.

(It rains. Fade out.)

Calling Time

By Michael West

Jack Lee, an older man, sits at a bar, nursing a pint.

His son, Gary, enters holding a mobile phone. He stands beside Jack.

Gary: Where's my pint?

Jack: You finished it.

Gary: No. It was full.

Jack: There was a dribble.

Gary: *(indicates a good half.)* There was that much.

Jack: It was gone. When I came back I'd this and he'd taken yours. It was empty.

(Gary suddenly smiles, trying to be a good sport.)

Gary: *(to unseen barman)* Another pint then, please. A full one this time.

(Gary sits and places his phone carefully before him.)

Gary: She said she enjoyed that.

Jack: Did she say that?

Gary: She said she enjoyed talking to you.

Jack: Is that why she rang?

Gary: She didn't ring. I rang her and said, "Talk to Dad." And handed you the phone and you handed it back to me and I was talking to her, and she said she enjoyed it. That's all I'm saying. I said to her, "Talk to your Old Man," and she said she would and she did and when I was talking to her after she said, "I enjoyed that."

Jack: Did she?

Gary: And why wouldn't she? It's not right not to talk to your Old Man, no matter what. *(Pause)* She lets herself be taken advantage of, Karen does. I'm always telling her: "Karen, you let people walk all over you." It upsets me. That, eh, fella she's living with.

Jack: What fella?

Gary: Ah, this fella.

Jack: Karen has a fella?

Gary: She's a good girl is Karen.

Jack: She is, she is. She didn't mention any fella to me.

Gary: You were only chatting for a minute.

Jack: I suppose.

Gary: You're not going to get all the news in one go, are you? She's hardly going to tell you her life story in 30 seconds. Where's that pint?

Jack: Is he all right?

Gary: *(to barman)* Excuse me. Can I have that pint please?

Jack: This fella. Is he all right?

Gary: No, that's what I'm saying.

Jack: He's not all right?

Gary: Ah, he's all right. He's ... It's the thing of, no one's good enough for my sister, you know?

Jack: What happened to ...?

Gary: Darren?

Jack: Was that him?

Gary: He was a waste. She's better off without him.

Jack: Darren. Is that his name?

Gary: Ah, he was a bollocks.

Jack: I must be thinking of someone.

*(**Gary's** pint arrives.)*

Gary: *(sternly)* Thank you. *(To **Jack**)* Whose round is this? I'll get it.

Jack: It's hardly a round if you just get yourself a pint.

Gary: My one was taken. I'm only ... I'm keeping you company.

Jack: Don't worry about it.

Gary: I'll get you a drink. You want a drink?

Jack: I'm fine.

Gary: I'll get you another.

Jack: I'm grand.

(Pause. They drink.)

Jack: I'm glad I talked to her. I'm glad she's ok.

Gary: She'll be fine if she gets rid of this fella.

*(**Gary** picks up his phone and starts texting.)*

Jack: There's this ... this eejit in the group session and he says, "We can't change the past. We can only change the future." And I says to him, "Bollocks. What about now? We live in the ... continuous present. That's all there is." I says to him, "Are you talking to me in the future? No. You're here talking to me now. And if you ask me tomorrow, or in ten years, I'll say ..."

*(**Gary** stands abruptly.)*

Gary: I'm going to ring her. Don't let them touch it. And you keep your hands to yourself.

Commiserations

By Niamh Creely

A woman sits on a sofa with a phone in her hand, crying. The TV is on and muted. She puts down the phone and wipes her eyes and her nose with a tissue. She sits still and closes her eyes for a moment. It's not easy, but she collects herself. She is suffering, but she has a job to do. She picks up the phone and calls a number.

Muirne: Ciara, hi, how are you. I just got a call from the hospital. Just after 6. Very peaceful. They're doing okay. We don't know the arrangements just yet, I'll probably be in touch tomorrow. I'm just ringing around now, letting everyone know. Yes. Thank you very much. Talk to you soon. Bye now.

(She calls another number.)

Muirne: Conor, hi there, how are you doing? How's the garage? Oh good, good, that's a great complaint! Great. I'm just giving you a quick call to let you know that Mary passed away just after 6 o' clock. It was a long time coming so, you know, it's a release. The kids are fine, they're being well looked after. So I'll be getting in touch with the arrangements probably tomorrow. Thank you very much, I'll pass that on. Talk to you soon. Bye now.

(She calls another number.)

Muirne: Ah, is that Johnny? Oh, Ciaran, hi. It's Muirne, I'm looking for your dad. Thank you. *(Pause)* Hi John, how are you? Sorry to disturb you, I'm sure you're watching the match now. *(laughs)* Well, we still have to support them anyway! Listen, John, I thought I'd give you a quick ring to let you know that Mary has passed away. Very peacefully, just after 6 this evening. Yes. So it was a release. They were all there, the kids got to say goodbye. No, no, I wasn't. They needed their space. *(John says, "Well it's all about family, isn't it?")* Yes, it is. It's all about family. Yes. Well, I'll be in touch with the arrangements. Probably tomorrow morning. Bye now.

(She calls another number.)

Muirne: Laura, hi, how are you? Do you have a minute? You're not in the middle of a feed or anything? Oh great, fantastic. I'm sure you're thrilled to have a bit of time to yourself. Oh, you're watching a film with himself? That's fantastic, sure you're spoiled! Well, I won't keep you but I'm afraid I have a bit of sad news. Mary has passed away. Yes, Mary Murphy, yes. No, I wasn't there but they said it was very peaceful, and they were all there together and the kids got to say goodbye and it was as good as it could have been, you know. Yes, yes. Oh, it's very sad. But she has the release now. And they have each other now, they're a very close-knit family, you know, and they'll get through it together. Thank you, I'll pass it on. *(A little surprised)* Oh, yes, she was a good friend.

*(**Muirne** tunes out of the conversation.)*

Muirne: *(covering up, a vast understatement)* I'll miss her.

(After a moment she catches herself and returns to the conversation.)

Muirne: OK, well I'll be letting you know the arrangements tomorrow, so I'll be in touch. All the best. And all the best to your boys, the two of them! Sorry? Oh, I'm grand. Don't be silly, not at all. Bye now, all the best.

(She puts down the phone beside her and stares into space for a moment. She rubs her eyes and unmutes the TV. Quiet canned laughter from a sitcom. Blackout.)

A Deal Made In Drimnagh

By Sean McLoughlin

Tony and Paula's front room, Friday night, Tony (early 20s) sits on his brown leather armchair drinking a bottle of beer, watching the television (a flat screen TV in the corner of the room). Paula (mid 20s) stands next to a coffee table in the middle of the room smoking a cigarette. There is a yellow Benson & Hedges ashtray close to the edge of the table. Because she is standing we can see that she 5 to 6 months pregnant, She looks upset.

Tony: Maybe if we were black and ... we were livin' in fuckin'... Los Angeles or somewhere like that. *(A beat)* But we're not black Paula. Nor do we live in Los Angeles. We live in Drimnagh!

Paula: Well then we'll give 'er a Drimnagh name.

Tony: Ahhh, now yer bein' silly.

(Paula looks away and takes a drag. A pause follows.)

Paula: It's a really nice name, Tony.

(Tony gives a small shake of his head.)

Tony: Made-up name.

Paula: Not a made-up name!

Tony: Tellin' ye, Paula....

Paula: French name!!! How many fucking times do I have to tell ye? *(**Tony** casually shakes his head no)* Beyonce! *(A beat)* That doesn't sound French to you?!

(Short pause.)

Tony: A bottle of champagne. *(A beat)* That's what it sounds like to me. *(**Paula** looks away in disgust.)* Or one of them spray things.

*(**Paula** takes a final drag from her cigarette, then bends down slowly to stab it out in the ashtray. **Paula** walks over to the couch, picks up her bottle of beer from the ground and slowly sits. She stares at the TV. After a few seconds **Tony** starts grinning. **Paula** notices.)*

Paula: What are ye grinnin' at? *(Not looking at **Paula**, **Tony** shakes his head. **Paula** looks back at the TV. A short pause follows.)* Still fuckin' grinnin'!

Tony: Relax, it's good.

Paula: What's good? I know *you're* good.

*(**Tony** shrugs off this last remark. Short pause.)*

Tony: Ye want to call the baby Beyonce, righ'?

*(**Paula** gives him a suspicious look.)*

Paula: *(slow)* Righ'.

*(**Tony** purses his lips and nods his head a couple of times.)*

Tony: I'll let ye call the baby Beyonce. *(A beat)* One condition though!

Paula: Wha'?!

(Short pause.)

Tony: Ye go back to bein' a peroxide blonde.

Paula: Awwww ... you are a sly one, aren't ye? You are a sly one. (*Tony nods his head yes.*) Burnin' the ear off me all summer about this. *(Short pause)* And when do ye want me to do this?

Tony: Soon as ye can. (*Paula laughs in desperation.*) Prefer it when yer blonde, Paula. What can I say?

Paula: Unbelievable.

Tony: That's the deal.

(Pause.)

(All of a sudden Paula's face lights up.)

Paula: I can't!

Tony: Wha'?

Paula: I can't do it!

(*Tony gawks at her.*)

Tony: Why can't ye do it?

Paula: Dangerous for the baby.

Tony: Would you ever ...

Paula: Seriously, Tony! All the chemicals and stuff. Could damage the baby.

Tony: You're just makin' that up.

Paula: I'm not, Tony. Honest to Jesus. You're not supposed to bleach yer hair when yer pregnant.

Tony: But it's perfectly all righ' to smoke?

Paula: Silk Cut Purple! Sure they're like smokin' air. *(Pause)* I'll bleach it after I've had the baby. What about that? *(**Tony** doesn't respond.)* That not good enough for ye?

*(**Tony** is thinking.)*

Tony: Bleach it once, before ye have the baby. *(A beat)* Now that's reasonable that is. Once isn't gonna do any damage to the baby.

(Short pause.)

Paula: After I have the baby.

Tony: Once, before ye have the baby.

*(**Paula** sighs.)*

Tony: Fuck ye, Tony. *(Short pause)*

Paula: Fuckin' months I was out of that thing!!!!!

Tony: What thing?

Paula: That ... fucking ... peroxide blonde thing!!

(Short pause.)

Tony: So do we have a deal here or wha'? *(**Paula** rolls her eyes.)* It's a good deal, Paula. *(A beat)* You get what you want, and I get what I want.

Paula: Pppph. Tony Soprana.

*(**Tony** shrugs.)*

Tony: Whatever. Do we have a deal?

(Short pause.)

Paula: Okay, fuck it. I'll bleach it then.

*(**Tony** claps his hands together and starts rubbing them.)*

Tony: Fair play to ye, Paula!

Paula: But you better not be spoofin' me about this!

Tony: No.

Paula: Coz I'm ringin' yer mother up now in a minute and tellin' 'er that this baby is gonna be called Beyonce. Then I'm gonna ring me own mother, then me sisters, then Elaine and Joanne. *(A beat)* So there's no gettin' out of it now.

Tony: Deal's a deal.

Paula: *(sarcastic)* Yeah.

*(Pause. A satisfied **Tony** takes a slug of his beer.)*

Tony: Beyonce really a French name?

Paula: Yeah!

Tony: Definitely not a made-up?

Paula: Fuck off, Tony!

*(**Paula** takes her cigarettes and lighter out of her nightgown pocket.)*

A Body

By Adrienne Michel Long

PERSONS: **Boy** – About 15 years of age.

The **Boy** is off stage. We just hear his voice, which comes from above.

SETTING: The bottom of Dublin's Grand Canal.

TIME: The action takes place now.

Darkness. A gentle light shines to reveal a stuffed black canvas bag downstage centre with the zip closed. Four feet above the black bag projected on the back wall is a subtle projection of a sliver of slightly rippled surface water.

Boy: *(OS)* Damsel flies and dragon flies hover overhead. Their larvae spent their youth clinging to the canvas of my case. At the brink of adulthood they left. I watched them shed their skin before they flew away. My own skin is shedding, but unlike my friends I will never fly.

I will always be fifteen.

I look down at my body, hidden four feet deep. I did not lose my way or stumble in. The depths of Dublin's Grand Canal was not my chosen grave. Nor is this suitcase. A coffin would have allowed me to outstretch my legs and lay back my head. Instead, I am bent, broken and bound inside the walls of this black bag.

My distended body fills every inch. Curled, foetal, still inside. Pond weeds, silt, ice outside. A rock is my sole accessory. It fixes me fast to the Canal floor. It hears my pleas and never moves.

My arms still bound. My lungs congealed. If I could utter one last word I'd expel the algae from every lobe and breathe in one last breath. I'd do this just to reveal his name, which sits at the tip of my engorged tongue. But I wouldn't want that. No, she wouldn't want that.

I see my face fading from my Missing poster above. My boyish features mixed with manhood. Stapled to a lamp-post, I'm smiling. If only it were a mirror. If only it were my face now. But my face is black and bloated and my eyes protrude. She can't see me now.

Even though the bruises are well disguised she'd get the picture pretty quick. The carnal remains of my half-naked body must never enter her maternal head. She'd realise the nightmare over and over. Why would I want to give her that?

It's better kept with me.

The coldness cools my rage, but there is nothing to soothe my loneliness. I must not think of my ma and she must not think of me.

A Body – Adrienne Michel Long

In time, the findings of my body should prove elusive. But this damn cold is holding things up. My organs have stopped decomposing. The maggots sleep in my gut, but a little warmth will wake them up. A mild spring will do wonders. With any luck, it will leave few leads: Just a body. Not a teenager. Not me.

(Fade to black.)

Dialogue

By Gregory Rosenstock

*Stage right, **Richman.***

*Stage left, **Poorman.***

They both hold a tin-can telephone, connected by a taut red ribbon.

Richman: *(can to mouth)* What?

Poorman: *(can to ear)* Help!

Richman: Speak up!

Poorman: Help!

Richman: Speak up! Speak up!

Poorman: Help! Help!

Richman: What do you want!

Poorman: Help!

*Enter **Politician** ceremoniously.*

He cuts the ribbon with scissors.

Round of applause.

Blackout.

BBC wartime signature tune repeated three times at short intervals, i.e., simulation of opening of Beethoven's 5th Symphony, played with bass drum.

Debris

By Evan Lee D'Alton

The family back garden, Friday evening. **Lizzie** *(mid 20s) is sitting on a bench and gazing absently at the sky. The UARS has re-entered the Earth's lower atmospheres and is expected to impact tonight. Her father (early 50s) has come out to join her, holding two mugs of tea.*

Dad: Ah. Your mother said you were out here (*sitting down*) Now, take this.

Lizzie: No, Dad, I'm OK. Really.

Dad: (*shrugs, putting her mug down on the ground beside him*) Suit yourself. (*Takes a sup of tea*)

Lizzie: I read that there's a satellite out there, just … falling. It's incredible, when you think about it. Six tonnes of … junk … just coming out of the sky.

Dad: Well. We best get on our helmets so.

(Lizzie *half-smiles.*)

Lizzie: I thought maybe I'd get to see it passing by.

(Short pause.)

Dad: Do you remember we got you that telescope when you were seven? And Christopher was jealous because it was him that wanted to be the astronaut? ... I told him there'd be two astronauts in *our* family.

Lizzie: *(smiling briefly)* Yeah. *(stopping)*

I didn't even want a telescope. I don't think I knew what a telescope was. Chris was always talking about that stuff, y'know?

(Pause.)

Dad: Are you sure you won't take your tea, love?

Lizzie: *(shaking head)* Thanks, Dad. I try not to have caffeine after 8 these days. It keeps me up.

Dad: Right. I see. Sure I suppose it's all coffee over there anyway ...

*(**Lizzie** leans forward and squints into the sky. It's nothing.)*

Dad: Lizzie, love *(stops, putting his hand on her knee)* – I'm glad you're home. We're all glad to see you back.

*(**Lizzie** ignores him, appearing somewhat uncomfortable.)*

Lizzie: Y'know, I read in the paper that there's a 1 in 22 trillion chance of getting hit by this thing. 22 trillion. Those are some pretty good odds.

Dad: Ah now. Knowing my bloody luck ...

Lizzie: *(swallows lump, getting more agitated)* That's the thing, though ... It's ... It's absolutely improbable, but it's not impossible is it?

Dad: *(shrugs)* Nothing's impossible, Lizzie.

Lizzie: No.

(*Pause.*)

It's funny. I mean, it won't hit us. But it could.

Dad: Lizzie –

Lizzie: Can you imagine, Dad? 22 *trillion.* You'd have to be (*voice breaks*) ... the unluckiest person in the known universe.

Lizzie: (*begins to sob;* **Dad** *puts his arm around her shoulder.*)

Dad: Now now. Come on, pet. It's OK.

Lizzie: (*through sobs*) I'm so sorry, Dad. I'm so sorry.

Dad: (*lump in his throat*) Don't be sorry, love. You've nothing to be sorry about. (*kisses her forehead*) It's not your fault. Christ, it isn't anybody's fault.

Lizzie: I should have been here ... if I'd known he was so bad ...

Dad: (*fighting back his own tears*) There was nothing you could have done. There was nothing anyone could have done. And you're here now, that's what matters. It's each other we need to be looking after now.

(**Lizzie** *sits up and wipes her tears from her face. She looks up at the sky, nodding her head.*)

Lizzie: We'll be OK, Dad. It'll be OK.

(**Lizzie** *takes his hand in hers.*)

Dad: We'll be fine.

(*Pause.* **Dad** *reaches forward for her mug.*)

Dad: Now get this tea into ya.

A Life

By Ronan Geoghegan

*Empty stage. A young **man** walks from stage right to stage centre. Floodlights hit him from the front; sound of a car, brakes
screeching. He turns quickly, eyes open in shock, and reacts to
oncoming car. Light becomes surreal, he becomes very still and
starts to speak.*

Man: Crawling quickly, butt wiggling ... Clutch the table top,
reach for big brother, hands touch, grasp, safe ... kick ball
scream with excitement ... running, chasing my cousins,
"I'll get you" ... Long carriage, blurry faces, moving too
fast, stomach churning, dinner angrily fighting its way
back up, skinny stranger's shoes turn chunky orange ...
Granddad J, croaky laugh, lovely sweets ... Mam and Dad
gone, car leaving without me, follow, shout loud, don't
hear, anxious fear, cry ... Mam cries, No more sweets from
Granddad ... itchy jumper but teenage mutant turtle bag,
big building, gangs of loud kids, no Mam or Dad today,
slightly worried but OK. ... Friendly faces, smiles offered,
shyly returned, "Hi, you want to play?", Friends, ... sit
on Granddad P's knee, he draws lions and dogs and tells

silly stories ... racing to the tree, tousled hair, excitement shaking to the bone under our cuddly pyjamas, rip paper, smash cardboard, "Look what I got" ... Dark night, long, black car, large, heavy box, Dad cries, aunties and Granny crying. Granddad P won't draw any more, he's gone to live with Granddad J ... Dad watching, we swing from the new trapeze in the hay shed ... I get sent to special teacher, "for an hour once a week is all, OK." ... stupid words, read yourselves, knuckles on head. "OWW" ... picking wild strawberries with Gram, eat them with milk and sugar "Mmm" ... Baby sister arrives, ecstatic ... "Who was in the special class last year?" Other idiots put up their hands, put mine in my pockets ... Going wild with Lisa Murphy and the rest of the football team, we won! ... Last day of school, should be happy, end of itchy green jumpers, instead sad ... new school! New teachers! Compensation new friends, Girls, beautiful ... In the hospital, Grams isn't well, we get the news, I know what it means now, tears come freely ... Sledding with my cousin Sean and my brothers, freezing but worth it, laughter ... first disco, wander through the crowd, girls and boys all over each other, nervous as hell ... sitting in my bedroom alone, reading, peaceful ... the class lock Mr Moran out of the room, detention, crap ... Disco, first sloppy, tongue twisting snog, not all it's cracked up to be ... climbing the school roof, detention ... First lesson on guitar, not as cool as I thought...failing to do religion project, detention ... Sports day, Running backwards to catch a ball, smash into something, Look up, a stunning face graciously accepts my stuttered apology ... Sitting in a class daydreaming about that girl ... Standing in a corner of a crowded room, heart racing, lungs shrinking, Watching pretty girl handing out sandwiches, how do I do this?! Slide along the wall, cheeks glowing red. "Hey", "Hey" the reply, hazel perfection taking me in. "Will you go to the debs with me" Shit, what happened to the small talk I'd planned! ... Dancing with her under the disco ball. Hold her close. Perfect moment ... Sit in the College grounds, her head on my knees ... Lying in bed, arms around pale white skin, heaven ... Buy some flowers and wine on my way to her apartment for her birthday, walk past a pub with the Pogues playing, step across the street, car screeching, lights blinding, "Katie!!"

(Lights and sound as at start. Blackout.)

The Nation's Assets

By Michelle Read

A couple in their thirties sit separately in smart leather armchairs facing the audience. They are having sex. They do not act this out, it is contained in their voices and the energy with which they sit forward – as if watching an exciting horse race. They are both wearing smart, high-fashion work suits.

Lights up.

Brian: Oh yeah … Yeah. Yeah baby … that's good.

Sinead: Oh yeah, that is good. Just like that, just like that.

Brian: Faster.

Sinead: Faster. Higher.

Brian: Higher.

Sinead: Push me.

Brian: Pull me. Go, go, go, go. That's right, girl, show me your assets.

Sinead: Yeeeaaah. *(pooped)* Phew, Jesus. Will we slow down for a bit?

Brian: I kinda like it fast.

Sinead: Yeah, fast is good, but baby, slow is good too.

Brian: Slow is nice, but fast is … fast is dynamic, go-getting, fast is speeding down the hill towards the …

Sinead: finishing line?

Brian: No, no, not that. No, towards the … next peak. Fast is about gaining momentum, seizing the day. Grabbing what's ours, going for it and not thinking about the consequences. Fast is abandoning ourselves to the ride. It's breakneck thrill-seeking, it's all-or-nothing … it's …

Sinead: how we ended up in an economic downturn.

Brian: Sinead!

Sinead: Oh Jesus, sorry.

Brian: How can I stay hard if you bring up the 'R' word. Shit!

Sinead: Quick, stop thinking about it.

Brian: Negative equity. Bollocks! Redundancies. Fuck!

Sinead: Come on, Brian, don't look back.

Brian: How else can we learn from our mistakes?

Sinead: You're a Celt, remember. The euro may come and go but you can weather any storm. You're a dirty great Celtic warrior striding up the valley… my valley, the valley of my mighty Celtic thighs.

Brian: Holding at 45 degrees. That's good, Sinead.

Sinead: Hang on in there, you can do it. Think of your bonus.

Brian: Oh yeah, talk dirty.

Sinead: Huge growth, hard currency, massive liquidity.

Brian: That's it, baby, the ISEQ Index is going back up.

Sinead: Oh my God, you're standing to attention.

Brian: Like a parade at the Áras. Like the fucking spire girl.

Sinead: That's what I call a great recovery.

Brian: I'm not beat yet.

Sinead: Fuck the begrudgers!

Brian: What? Who's been talking behind my back?

Sinead: Focus, Brian. We've still got a job to do. Stay on target. Yeah, that target. Oh. Oh. Oh. Yeah, Brian, that's it.

Brian: You are a very bold girl.

Sinead: Don't I know it.

Brian: Spending money like water.

Sinead: I couldn't help myself, Brian. Fourteen store cards.

Brian: And all of them maxed out.

Sinead: I was rolling in credit.

Brian: You dirty borrower.

Sinead: But now I'm sorry.

Brian: Oh baby, you're so contrite.

Sinead: You just have to look at me and I'm contrite.

Brian: Oh yeah. Oh yeah, oh yeah, baby!

Sinead: Wait! Wait!

Brian: Shit.

Sinead: WAIT A MINUTE!

Brian: I'm trying.

Sinead: Oh no you don't.

Brian: I think I'm over extended.

Sinead: Angela Merkel.

Brian: What?

Sinead: Christine Lagarde.

Brian: What are you doing?

Sinead: I'm getting on top with the big girls.

Brian: Ow!

Sinead: I'm taking over!

Brian: I feel dizzy, Sinead.

Sinead: A firm hand on the reigns.

Brian: Janey!

Sinead: We're going to shake off the old positions, Brian. We've got to buck the trends.

Brian: Ah!

Sinead: Thrust forward.

Brian: Ah!

Sinead: Play the long game.

Brian: Jesus.

Sinead: Work at our stamina.

Brian: Oh Christ.

Sinead: Pull together.

Brian: Ah.

Sinead: Yeah baby that's it … that's it, until we achieve a long-term, sustainable, mutual, viable … Aaaahhhhhggggg!

*(**Sinead** recovers like a cat who got the cream. She sits back in her seat, spent.)*

Sinead: Good man. We should probably get back to work.

Brian: Right, Yeah.

Sinead: The nation's assets aren't going to manage themselves.

Tuesday Evening (*Following The News*)

By Darren Donohue

*Lights come up revealing a kitchen/living-room containing an oven (stage left), a table (centre stage), a chair (stage right); a stack of slates also sit downstage right. **Charlie** (thirties) stands centre stage in his pyjamas holding a large butterfly net and intensely watching the sky. His wife, **Steph**, (thirties) enters wearing a smart suit.*

Steph: *(dejected)* Hi, honey, I'm home.

Charlie: Hi, love. How was work?

Steph: Terrible. I was forced to take voluntary redundancy.

Charlie: What?

Steph: A HR posse ambushed me after lunch.

Charlie: No!

Steph: They pinned me against the wall, produced a shotgun and *suggested* I take voluntary redundancy.

Charlie: What did you say?

Steph: I couldn't really speak with the barrel in my mouth so I just signed the papers.

Charlie: I don't know what the world is coming to!

Steph: How was your day?

Charlie: A disaster! Look at the roof.

Steph: (*looking up*) Oh no!

Charlie: Around twelve the slates began rattling and shaking loose. By the time I climbed into the attic they were circling the house like a flock of pigeons.

Steph: Where are they now?

Charlie: I don't know. This enormous slate cloud appeared, gobbled them up and took off. I managed to net a few stragglers but I'm not sure they're ours.

Steph: (*sighs*) Nothing we can do about it tonight. I'll get a start on dinner.

Charlie: All right, love, I'll set the table.

(**Steph** *moves to the oven, switches it on and we hear a sound of gas. She opens the oven door and sticks her head inside.* **Charlie** *discards his net and sits. He finds a hangman's noose and fiddles with the knot.* **Steph** *suddenly whips her head out of the oven and switches it off.*)

Steph: I forgot to pick up the children!

Charlie: Where are they?

Steph: At the crèche.

Charlie: We'll collect them tomorrow.

Steph: Do they keep children there overnight?

Charlie: *(laughs)* Of course not. *(Serious)* They take them home.

Steph: Home?

Charlie: To their house.

Steph: Won't they miss us?

Charlie: You know how much they love sleepovers. Anyway, it'll give us a break, a chance to unwind.

Steph: I do feel a little tense.

Charlie: There you go then. Let's make the most of it.

Steph: All right.

*(**Steph** switches back on the oven and sticks her head inside.)*

Charlie: There's some post on the table, dear.

*(**Steph** switches off the oven, moves to the table and flicks through the letters.)*

Steph: Bill. Bill. Bill. *(Worried)* Bank statement.

Charlie: What's wrong?

Steph: *(considering the envelope)* Says here there's an extra charge if we open it.

Charlie: How would they know if we opened it?

Steph: Doesn't say.

Charlie: What's the charge?

Steph: A percentage of our savings.

Charlie: Ha! We don't have any savings.

Steph: *(reading)* "If sufficient funds are unavailable in 'said' account a swift and brutal retribution shall be visited upon 'named' account holders. This punishment involves a hose and rubber gloves."

Charlie: Why can't they ever say what they mean!

Steph: What will I do?

Charlie: Better not risk it. It's probably hooked up to the internet somehow.

*(**Steph** comes downstage holding a large, golden envelope.)*

Steph: What's this?

Charlie: I missed that one.

Steph: It says, *Handle With Care.*

Charlie: *(moving to **Steph**)* Perhaps we've won something.

*(**Steph** rips open the envelope and finds two long, colourful feathers. Charlie takes one of them.)*

Charlie: *(astonished)* They're still perfect!

Steph: More beautiful than ever!

Charlie: But I remember selling it!

Steph: I gave mine away!

Charlie: So what are they doing here?

Steph: Maybe some things can't be given away or sold.

*(**Charlie** and **Steph** face out and place the feathers ceremoniously behind their heads. They take deep breaths and let out a terrifying Indian war cry. Blackout.)*

The Audition

By Rory Nolan

*A busy pub. Music, but the chat is louder. **Melissa** (39) is standing holding a glass of red wine. **Hughie** (35), well on his way, holding a half-drunk pint of Guinness and grinning from a just-finished conversation, backs into her. Upsets both drinks. The following conversation is pitched slightly above the music and general ambience. Hyphens indicate overlapping speech.*

Hughie: Shit, sorry. *(Beat)* Jesus. Melissa Harty. *(Beat)* There y' are now.

Melissa: *(one slow nod)* Here I am, Hughie French. *(Beat)* Well done tonight.

Hughie: Ah thanks, ye know sure -

Melissa: Great-

Hughie: Shakespeare's-

Melissa: -take.

Hughie: -the bomb ... which?

Melissa: *(louder)* Nothing. *(Beat)* Good job tonight. A bomb?

Hughie: *(Beat)* Thanks. Yeah.

(Pause.)

Melissa: So. We'll be seeing you tomorrow?

Hughie: Affirmative, that's right, yes indeed, Melissa. Quarter past twelve.

Melissa: *(nods in agreement)* Quarter to twelve. The Exchequer.

Hughie: *(Beat)* Can't wait. *(Beat)* Hope the hum of drink off me doesn't fog the camera! Ha!

Melissa: *(Beat)* Sure. *(Beat)* Hope so too.

(Pause.)

Hughie: How's Adam?

Melissa: Adam?

Hughie: Yeah. The hubby. *(Beat)* Fiancé?

Melissa: Fiancé.

Hughie: Fiancé. *(Beat)* Anyway, his Othello was *amazing*.

Melissa: Yeah. He was great.

Hughie: And no need to black up! Ha ha ha! *(Beat)* – *(**Melissa** looks at **Hughie**, trying to gauge his self-awareness.)* You cast it, right?

Melissa: *(Beat)* I did.

Hughie: Friends in high places, wha'!? Ha!

(Pause.)

Hughie: Tricky role, the fear gorm.

Melissa: What?

Hughie: *(louder)* The fear gorm.

Melissa: Angry?

Hughie: Sorry?

Melissa: Did you say you're angry-

Hughie: Who-

Melissa: -in Irish? *(Beat)* Tá fearg orm?

Hughie: Yes. Irish. Black fellah. Well. Blue.

Melissa: Blue?

Hughie: That's what the Irish is.

Melissa: I know. Is it not a bit-

Hughie: Funny that.

Melissa: -racist?

*(**Hughie** doesn't hear this. Nods affirmatively. Beat.)*

Melissa: I've probably got that wrong. No Irish, me.

(Pause.)

Hughie: Fuck. Sorry. How insensitive of me. You're having a baby, right?

(Beat.)

Melissa: Had it.

(Beat.)

Hughie: You and Adam! Parents. You guys? Wow.

(Beat.)

Melissa: Yeah.

Hughie: Crazy!

Melissa: Just ... Well. Crazy.

(Pause.)

Hughie: What did ye have?

Melissa: What? When?

Hughie: A boy or a girl, like?

Melissa: A girl, Hughie.

Hughie: A girl! Wow! What d'ye call 'er?

Melissa: *(Beat. Grimaces. Sure she's misheard.)* Em. Sorry?

Hughie: *(louder)* WHA' D'YE CALL 'ER?

Melissa: *(Pause. Stares at Hughie. Answers, icily)* Black.

Hughie: What?!

Melissa: Black.

(Beat.)

Hughie: Black?? BLACK!! What kind of a name is ....? You are fuckin' mad, Melissa Harty, you know that? *(Beat)* Black! Ha ha!

Melissa: Yes, Hughie. My baby is black.

Hughie: *(Beat, dawns)* Jesus. No. No. I mean, I don't care what the baby ... Jesus Melissa, not the colour ... in that ... I don't ... I don't care what colour ... I'm not a -

Melissa: I have to go.

(Music changes song. Momentary lull in ambiance.)

Hughie: - racist.

(Beat.)

Melissa: Bye, Hughie.

(Music back up.)

Hughie: No! *(Grabs her by arm)* I said, "What. did. you. call. her. As in her name. *(On exhalation)* Jesus.

Melissa: *(dawns)* Oh. Em. Rose.

Hughie: *(relieved sigh)* Rose. Lovely. Red Rose. Ha. Or white. *(beat)* Or-

Melissa: See you tomorrow, Hughie.

Hughie: - whatever. Yeah. Bye, Melissa. Quarter past twelve.

Melissa: *(nods affirmatively)* Quarter to twelve.

*(Exit **Melissa**. **Hughie** blows through his lips. Enter **Liam** carrying two double whiskeys.)*

Liam: Hughie Boy, here's to the best Second Gravedigger I've ever seen, I mean that now. Get that into you. Who was that?

Hughie: *(gaze is fixed on **Melissa** as she walks out)* Cheers. Melissa Harty. Casting director.

Liam: She's casting that big Russian thing, yeah?

Hughie: I know. I'm in for it tomorrow.

Liam: Nice. What's it like?

Hughie: *(back to **Liam**)* Yeah, deadly. *(Beat)* But not my cup of tea. *(Beat)* And I'm totally wrong for the part.

(Lights.)

Guaranteed Irish

By Colin Murphy

Cast: **The Taoiseach**, **The Minister for Finance**, *and an* **Aide**. *All are male.*

Note: These are not to be played as if impersonating actual politicians.

Setting: Government buildings; the present, or thereabouts.

A room of State, in the middle of the night. **The Taoiseach** *and* **Minister for Finance** *sit in armchairs. They are pensive. Silence. The door opens. An* **Aide** *enters. He is exhausted.* **The Minister for Finance** *pays him no attention.*

Taoiseach: Well?

Aide: Yes.

Taoiseach: All of them?

Aide: Yes.

Taoiseach: Even?

Aide: Yes.

Taoiseach: Where the fuck was he?

Aide: His phone was dead. We had to send a guard around to his house.

Taoiseach: They're waiting?

Aide: Yes.

Taoiseach: Christ.

(He has a sudden need for a cigarette. He takes out one and lights it.)

Aide: Eh, Taoiseach—

Taoiseach: What?

Aide: You can't—

Taoiseach: To paraphrase one of my less illustrious predecessors: a cigarette or a transfer; to Limerick?

*(**Aide** takes a cigarette and leaves. **Finance** takes a clove of garlic from a pocket and peels it. They lapse into silence.)*

Taoiseach: Let's go through it again.

Finance: Again?

Taoiseach: One more time.

Finance: *(Gestures to suggest he'll set out both sides of the argument.)* So, Hiberno is empty. It's been frozen. In the morning when the markets realise, it's going to collapse. There may be a panic. A run on the banks. Hiberno brings down the others, it's a perfect storm: the public demanding their money, the share price collapsing, and the interbank market closing to Irish banks. The entire banking system freezes. No one gets paid. The economy could collapse, and they'll blame us because we didn't do anything to stop it. They'll say we should have guaranteed them.

Taoiseach: And the other side.

Finance: We guarantee them. So there's no liquidity problem – no panic. That gets us through this week. But then we discover it wasn't just a liquidity problem: Hiberno is bust.

Taoiseach: It's not bust.

Finance: Let's just say. Worst case scenario: they're lying, it's bust. So Hiberno goes down, but we've guaranteed it, so we're on the hook – and that's not just for deposits. The bondholders too. *(Beat)* Ten billion. Maybe fifteen. Hiberno sends shockwaves through the rest. The bond yields shoot up. It takes us three years of austerity budgets to get fully out of it. And they'll blame us. They'll say we shouldn't have guaranteed it.

Taoiseach: Ten to fifteen billion.

Finance: Worst case.

Taoiseach: It's pretty fucking bad.

(They lapse into silence.)

Finance: Bancus ruptus.

Taoiseach: What?

Finance: Ruptus – broken. Bancus –

*(**Aide** enters.)*

Taoiseach: A bank. I got it.

Finance: A bench. A broken bench. Bankers used to just be fellows on benches in markets. Handing out cash. When they went bust, they just broke the bench.

Aide: What if the bench was systemic?

(Silence. They look at him.)

Aide: Sorry. *(Beat)* Eh. The time—

Finance: We know.

Aide: The Asian markets-

Taoiseach: We know.

Aide: half an hour-

Taoiseach: We've got it.

*(**Aide** leaves. Silence)*

Taoiseach: What's the worst that could happen?

Finance: *(serious)* Riots. Bloodshed. *(With grim humour)* A coup.

Taoiseach: The worst in which case?

Finance: Both cases.

(Beat.)

Taoiseach: *(with a new sense of calm decisiveness)* Have you a coin?

Finance: What?

Taoiseach: Have you a coin?

Finance: *(checks his pockets)* No.

Taoiseach: Minister for fucking Finance doesn't have a fucking coin!

Aide: Taoiseach.

Taoiseach: *(aggressively)* What?

Aide: Taoiseach, a coin, Taoiseach.

*(He gives it to **The Taoiseach**.)*

Taoiseach: That'll be all, Richard.

Aide: Taoiseach –

Taoiseach: That'll be all!

*(**Aide** leaves. **Taoiseach** looks **Finance** in the eye. Beat.)*

Taoiseach: Are you ready?

*(**Finance** nods. **Taoiseach** goes to flip the coin, but stops.)*

Taoiseach: Which is it?

Finance: Which?

Taoiseach: Either.

Finance: Harp.

Taoiseach: Which?

Finance: The guarantee.

(Beat.)

Taoiseach: Harp, ten to fifteen billion.

Finance: Or nothing at all if it works.

Taoiseach: Heads, on their own heads be it, they're on their own. *(Beat)* Are you ready? *(Beat. **Taoiseach** makes to flip a coin, high. Catches coin and holds it covered on the back of his hand.)*

Finance: *(whispers)* Christ.

(Lights out.

End.)

It's A Lovely Day, Bill Withers

By Jody O'Neill

*A **man** is sitting at a desk. On the desk are piles of bills. On the floor are piles of bills. Hanging from the ceiling are more bills.*

*This **man** is drowning in debt.*

*The **man** sits. He is paralysed. Doesn't know where to begin.*

*The **man** moves a pile of bills, so that it is in front of him.*

He opens one, throws the envelope in a bin beside him, lays the bill on the floor.

He opens another one, throws the envelope in a bin beside him, lays the bill on the floor.

Another …

And another …

*And another, another, another, another, another, until the bills make a carpet around the **man** and his desk.*

*A **woman** enters. She watches the **man**. The man is unaware of her presence and continues his task.*

Another ...

And another ...

And another and another and –

*The **woman** reaches over his shoulder. Takes the bill he is about to put on the ground. Doesn't let go of his hand.*

Sings very quietly ...

When I wake up in the morning, Love.

The man can't let go of her hand.

***Woman** keeps singing.*

And the sunlight hurts my eyes.

And something without warning, Love.

She pulls the man to his feet. They embrace.

Bears heavy on my mind.

They are dancing, a slow, uncertain, unsteady dance on top of the carpet of debt.

*The **woman** is humming the tune.*

They keep dancing.

She gets stuck on repeat.

When the day that lies ahead of me,

Seems impossible to face.

When the day that lies ahead of me,

Seems impossible to face.

When the day that lies ahead of me,

Seems impossible to face.

They rest their heads on each other's shoulders, still dancing.

When the day that lies ahead of me,

Seems impossible to face.

When the day that lies ahead of me,

Seems impossible to face.

LFX: The dance continues as the lights fade to dark. The white bills glow in the darkness, even when we can't see the couple any-more.

Sure This Is It

By Ciara Ní Chuirc

Two girls sit in a car park, sharing a plastic bottle of cider. It is 3 a.m. **C** *chugs while* **K** *lists words beginning with the letter L.*

K: Llllline. Limp. Limpet. Livid. Licks. Lick*ing*. Lips. Love. Life. Llllllinger. Loop. Looping. Loops. Eh ...

C: *(stops drinking)* You hesitated! My turn! *(Hands* **K** *the bottle)* Okay, M. M, M, M.

K: I'm bored of this. Let's stop playing.

C: Wimp.

K: Whatever. You're a drunk. Anyway, we got all the way to L. That's like half the alphabet. Sure sign we're alcoholics.

C: Someday we'll get to Z.

K: Yeah, and then we'll get alcohol poisoning.

C: Whatever.

K: Whatever. *(Drinks)*

C: We really have to stop drinking in car parks.

K: Yeah.

C: Yeah. *(Drinks)*

K: We really have to get our shit together.

C: Yeah.

K: Yeah. *(Drinks)*

C: We really do.

K: What are you gonna do?

C: After college?

K: Yeah.

C: Fuck knows. *(Drinks)*

K: Ha. Yeah.

C: *(decisively)* Go away. I'm gonna go away.

K: Yeah?

C: This country ... this *fucking* country ... I hate it here. It's so ... narrow. I can't stay here.

K: Way to be melodramatic. Ireland's not so bad.

C: Are you gonna stay here?

K: Oh God no. Stay here? And do what? No jobs. No money. This country's a shithole. *(Drinks)*

C: *(laughs)* It sure is.

K: Where do you wanna go?

C: The States probably. I don't know. New York. San Fran. Anywhere but here. What about you? *(Drinks)*

K: Hmmm ... Norway.

C: *(chokes with laughter, coughs)* Norway?

K: Yeah, Norway!

C: Norway ... *(Drinks)*

K: What's wrong with Norway?

C: Huh ... nothing.

K: What?

C: I mean ... Norway? For real?

K: Yeah. So?

C: But ... why? You don't speak Norwegian.

K: Yeah, well, I'll learn, won't I, when I'm there like.

C: What would you do there?

K: Dunno. Work. And ... drink. *(drinks)* And eat ... like, little strudels and Norwegian foods. And look at fjords. You know. Do Norwegian things.

C: Um ...

K: Shut up! I'll meet a man, called like Sven or something. We'll get married and have lots of blonde-haired, blue-eyed children, and call them-

C: Isn't that Sweden?

K: What?

C: Blonde hair and blue eyes? Isn't that Sweden?

K: Whatever.

C: Also you're not blonde haired. Or blue eyed, for that matter.

K: WHATEVER. Sven will have blonde hair and blue eyes. Stop shitting all over my future.

C: It's kind of stupid.

K: No it isn't. *You're* kind of stupid.

C: Oh, good one. *(Drinks)*

(Pause onstage.)

Unrequited

By Michael Cussen

*George and **Phonsie** seated on milking stools and back to back, just a yard of space between them. They are in a darkened-out milking parlour. (We may / may not see their hands stretching out in front of them as they hand milk a cow each. They may be preparing for the milking or just taking a break while sitting on the milking stools if the foregoing concept does not work). The electricity has broken down, and the two men are returned to times past. There are dusty high-up windows through which some light is visible, but in general they are in twilight. Each man has a tin bucket for the milk between his knees.*

Phonsie: When did the standby generator break down?

George: Same time as the electric.

Phonsie: Isn't that the way! Get one flat tyre, get two.

The last time . . .

George: What's that, Phonsie?

Phonsie: The last time we milked by hand. I'd say . . . I'd say sixty-eight.

George: Earlier.

Phonsie: Earlier?

George: Sixty-six.

Phonsie: Sixty-six?

George: Still it's like – anything. You never forget.

Phonsie: What?

George: The milking. Wasn't it grand the chats we used to have.

Milk a cow, have a fag, milk a cow, have a chat, finish the milking . . .

Phonsie: In for the tay.

George: The easygoing way. We were working away, and still . . .

Phonsie: And still.

George: What?

Phonsie: What?

George: You said "still" like you were thinking of something.

Phonsie: Yeah. I was. I was thinking of Mary Maguire.

George: *(stops)* Mary? Oh, yes. Mary Maguire.

Phonsie: Whatever put Mary into my head . . .

George: The long ago conversation I suppose. The dark. The things you see in your head in the dark. Like Mary Maguire.

She was some – some looking . . .

Phonsie: Dame.

George: She was some looking . . . .

Phonsie: She was some looking woman, George.

George: She was and all. She was some looking woman.

The lovely dark tresses of her . . . .

Phonsie: And her face. A true face. Not a scowl, not a smirk. A beautiful . .

George: A beautiful . . .

Phonsie: Beautiful face.

(*Pause.*)

Phonsie: And her figure

George: She had some beautiful . . .

Phonsie: Beautiful figure . . . I used to imagine what it must have been like to have my arm around Mary Maguire and I sailing around the ballroom with Brendan Bowyer lashing out the music.

George: *(stops)* But sure . . .

Phonsie: What?

George: Nothing.

(*George recommences milking. Pause onstage.*)

Sure This Is It (cont.)

C: So that's your plan?

K: Yeah.

C: Well ... great.

K: Forget it. It's a stupid plan.

C: No, it's ... it's a good plan.

K: It isn't. *(Pause. Drinks.)* What are you gonna do in the States?

C: Dunno. Maybe if I go there something will happen.

K: What kind of thing?

C: Anything.

K: Well, that's not much of a plan.

C: Says you!

K: What?

C: At least I'm not going to Sweden to start the Hitler Youth.

K. NORWAY. I'm going to NORWAY.

C: *(tilts bottle)* This is gone.

K: Thank fuck; I'm freezing. Let's go home.

(She pulls **C** *up.)*

C: We're gonna get out of here, right?

K: Of course we are.

(She goes to leave, **C** *stops her by grabbing her arm.)*

C: I mean ... I just ... more than anything, I want my life to start. I want something ... anything ... to happen.

(Pause.)

C: I need my life to start.

(Pause.)

K: That's pretty wanky.

(They laugh, and exit.)

(End of play.)

Unrequited (cont.)

Phonsie: I do miss it, George. The way we were before.

George: Before?

Phonsie: Before we all stopped smokin' and goin' to the pub and . . .

George: . . . having a bit of a life.

Phonsie: A bit of a life.

What was so bad that they banned them all on us?

Were they so terrible that they couldn't leave us a couple of simple little things?

George: And I wouldn't mind but all the time that crowd . . .

Phonsie: . . . that lousy crowd up there. . .

George: . . . were workin' night and day to sink the whole country . . .

*(Silence. **George** stops.)*

George: *(stops)* Phonsie?

Phonsie: *(stops)* Yeah?

George: She was your girl, you know? She was for you, Phonsie.

Phonsie: For me? Oh, no, George, it was you she liked . . .

George: *(taken aback)* Is that what you thought?

Phonsie: Of course it was.

George: *(stands)* Ah, no, Phonsie. I'd see the way she looked at you.

She never looked at me that way.

Phonsie: *(stands)* But why would she want me? I didn't have an acre.

I had nothing going for me, George . . .

George: Maybe she didn't look at things that way.

(Pause.)

Phonsie: *(as the penny drops)* So – I thought she was yours, and . . . *(She was mine.)*

*(**George** and **Phonsie** look at one another, horrified by the discovery. **Phonsie** is especially shocked by the news. Glumly they return to work.)*

Phonsie: When will the ESB be back?

George: They said tomorrow.

Phonsie: Tomorrow.

George: Tomorrow, Phonsie.

Phonsie: About Mary Maguire . . .

*(**George** stops milking and looks up to where **Phonsie** is standing.)*

George: We made an awful balls of that, Phonsie.

(Silence, then sadly.)

Phonsie: Yes, George. I suppose we did.

(Lights down.)

(End of play.)

Where Will We Go?

By Dermot Bolger

This playlet occurs when it appears that the evening of plays is over. The cast of the previous playlet have left the stage and stage-hands enter to seemingly dismantle the set. They bring on a ladder, hammers and saws, but work noiselessly, unobtrusively. An actress rises from the end seat as the stage-hands enter, her timing letting the audience quickly grasp that she is a part of the play. As she speaks she holds the audience with her gaze, while quietly making her way to mount the steps to the stage. On stage she briefly observes and moves among the stage-hands, who seem oblivious to her.

Actress: Where will we go now, when we are not truly dead, but no longer live inside some actress; when we are condemned to be locked away inside the pages of an old script? When carpenters strike the set, when we have no borrowed body to inhabit; no stolen voice to allow us say those things we desperately needed to say on the night we entered a playwright's imagination as they drifted towards sleep; when we demanded they switch back on the bedroom light and find a pen to let us speak; when we refused to stop haunting them until we made ourselves heard.

You – the audience – can simply go home. But we are trapped in the limbo we created when we indentured ourselves as phantoms of their imaginations. The writers knew our names the moment they began to write in bed or searched for a notebook when stopped at traffic lights. We ambushed them. One moment we did not exist; the next moment they knew every intonation of our voice, our past stories, our ultimate fates. We haunted them till they wrote us down – like we have haunted you all evening, demanding you too play your part in giving purpose to our unlived existences.

(Reaching the stage, she looks back at the audience.)

It was all make-believe, a fantasy that felt real because people in the next seats seemed to invest credence in us too. But leave now. You've played your part: you were fed fables you chose to believe. Leave with the stage-hands and bar staff. Only we belong here after the lights go out. We wait here like the inhabitants of a ghost estate on the edge of a flood plain: apparently a place but not really a place because it exists on no map.

These lands we conjured never existed except during the brief seconds when you loaned us your belief so we could materialise, like unexplained presences at a séance: seemingly real because everyone held their breath and suspended disbelief. But sadly it was a three-card conman's trick. So blink now in the house lights, realise you were collectively fooled again. Drive home past abandoned apartment blocks, roads petering out into nowhere. These are the backdrop to the greatest feat of theatre you ever saw: where magicians produced rabbits from hats, illusions so grandiose no playwright could dare invent them.

It's time we all disappeared now, like people's money and dreams. A part of us goes home inside you, to exist only in your remembrance; another part of us lives on in the memory of the actors who played us. But in truth we're trapped here, our voices flitting like bats between the fly-lofts after everyone has left. We wait here for you to let us live again, to gather strength from your empathy, your need to let yourself be seduced, to surrender your trust and believe again in lies being fed to you by confidence-tricksters, leaders and playwrights; by fabulous, unobtainable illusions that, like us, suddenly appear to be here, then, just as suddenly, are gone.

(She exits. Lights go down on stage-hands.)

TINY PLAYS FOR IRELAND 2

Credits | Tiny Plays For Ireland 2

Tiny Plays for Ireland 2 were first produced by Fishamble: The New Play Company on 12 March 2013 at the Project Arts Centre, Dublin with the following cast and production team:

Man 1	**Peter Daly**
Man 2	**Don Wycherley**
Man 3	**Steve Blount**
Woman 1	**Mary Murray**
Woman 2	**Sorcha Fox**
Director	**Jim Culleton**
Dramaturgy	**Gavin Kostick**
Set Designer	**Sabine Dargent**
Costume Designer	**Niamh Lunny**
Lighting Designer	**Paul Keogan**
Sound Designers	**Ivan Birthistle and Vincent Doherty**
Producer	**Marketa Dowling**

PR	**Sinead O'Doherty at Gerry Lundberg PR**
Production Manager	**Des Kenny**
Stage Director	**Paula Tierney**
Stage Manager	**Clare Howe**
Hair & Make-Up	**Val Sherlock**
Graphic Designer	**Dave Darcy**
Stills	**Pat Redmond**
Production Assistant	**Jessica Carri**
Assistant Director	**Sarah Finlay**

Running Order | Tiny Plays For Ireland 2

Tiny Plays For Ireland

The Night Feed by Justine Mitchell

Light at the End of the Tunnel by Eleanor White

Naked Photographs of My Mother by Brendan Griffin

The Cost of Your Forgetting by Henry Martin

I Stand Here Before You by Tom Swift

Positive Protest by Christine McKeon

The Caring Ireland, 2013 by Pauline McLynn

Life in 2 Syllables by Mike Finn

Slanesman by Colum McCann

Somewhere

By Mark Cantan

Narrator: Somewhere in Ireland right now ...

A baker gets the feeling he's been written into the wrong genre.

A politician worries about offending homophobes.

A young woman is unsure whether to shake the hand of a priest.

A horticulturalist realises he's been mispronouncing the word mispronunciation.

A young couple worry they might some day run out of things to say to each other like the old couple sitting across the restaurant from them.

A man types his country as Ireland while ordering an Obama t-shirt from China.

A little girl sees a cow for the first time. She calls it "Dada".

An old couple enjoy playing a game where they sit silently in a restaurant to freak out young couples sitting across the restaurant from them.

A woman gets to grips with differentiation, 37 years too late for her exams.

A wedding service pauses for an ad break.

A cartographer mixes up East and West for the 657th time.

Two biologists touch eating holes.

On a ferry entering the harbour a 9-year-old boy slaps the bald head of a man he has mistaken for his father.

The worshippers of a Bronze Age god run a schooling system.

A woman challenges her friend to read the obituaries aloud without laughing.

A duck bobs.

Fond memories fill a man's thoughts as his wife apologises for beans on toast for dinner.

A consultant stares at an X-ray, wondering why they all look like dragons to him.

Taxi drivers march on government to protest the introduction of students' fees.

A young woman wonders if things will ever change. A middle-aged woman wonders if things will ever be the same. An old woman wonders whose turn it is to deal.

For the first and only time a young man tries to speed up his morning routine by brushing his teeth while sitting on the toilet.

An actuary calculates the miniscule probability that she was ever born and promptly dies.

A high court judge cringes at the memory of accidentally calling his 6th class teacher Miss Orgasm.

A 30-year-old shopper feels uncomfortable being called Sir by a 60-year-old shop assistant.

A committee come to a decision none of them is happy with.

A jockey lets his horse win this one.

The static electricity from the rubbing together of two hipster lovers' woollen jumpers short circuits their Sodastream.

A young boy discovers what happens when you "pull someone's finger".

An old couple fall in love.

An egg is fertilised, but the little boy who planted it is mistaken in thinking it will grow a chicken tree.

Misreading a recipe a woman invents shepherd's gratin.

A roadie promises to be faithful to his cheating wife.

A security guard plans a surprise funeral.

A man checks the bus timetable and then waits the same amount of time as he would have had he not checked it.

Seeing the red light a little too late a man stops his car in the middle of a pedestrian crossing, blocking it.

A blind woman doesn't realise she has a photographic memory.

A drunk man slurs an unintelligible list of the causes he'd give his life for.

A man wonders at the number of his female friends that sign off their texts with the pseudonym 'x'.

Two campaigners see each other's side of the argument.

A woman's horoscope successfully predicts that she'll keep reading her horoscopes.

A "Please ensure that this door remains shut" sign is ignored.

A fight breaks out in a schoolyard over whose child is the strongest.

And a group of people wonder what could be happening somewhere in Ireland right now.

Grand Canal Dock

By Tanya Wilson

This is a true event that I recently experienced:

Grand Canal Dock, Monday morning. A **Man** *in a business suit clings to the side of a footbridge. A* **Girl** *in her twenties approaches, pushing a bike.*

Girl: What are you doing in the water?

Man: I'm sorry, I just tried to kill myself …

Girl: What?! Why would you do that!

(She takes hold of his hand.)

Man: I can't swim.

Girl: Jesus! Can you pull yourself over to the wall, I can't hold you.

Man: I'm trying to, I'm so cold, please help me.

Girl: I can't take your weight, you're too heavy for me to hold, what should I do? I don't know what to do! *(Shouts)* HELP!

(Frantically looking around)
Please someone help!

Man: I'm sorry.

Girl: It's all right, you just need to pull yourself across; I can't help you from here. Can you touch the bottom?

Man: No, it's too deep ...

(He slips from her grasp, she struggles as he nearly pulls her in.)

Girl: Stop! You're pulling me in ... I can't hold you, I'm not strong enough.

Man: Don't let go, please. I can't swim.

Girl: I'm sorry, I can't ...

(A man in his twenties arrives on his bike.)

Young Man: Are you all right there?

Girl: Oh God, please help, he tried to kill himself!

Young Man: *(to Man)* It's all right mate, we'll get you out. You must be freezing in there!

(To Girl) Ring an ambulance.

Girl: OK ... 999 yeah?

Young Man: Yes!

Girl: I'm sorry, I can't think straight.

Man: I can't swim, please ...

Young Man: Take my hand, I'm going to pull you across and you should be able to climb out, what's your name?

Girl: Hi! Yeah, I need an ambulance ...

Man: Andrew ...

Girl: There's a man in the water, he tried to kill himself ...

Young Man: *(pulling him)* That's it, keep going, nearly there.

Girl: Grand Canal Dock, the footbridges over the water … yeah he's soaked, his lips are blue … I don't know, he was in the water when I arrived, another man's pulling him out now … yes, three of us including him … no, there's no one else around … please hurry.

*(To **Man**)* How old are you?

Man: Thirty-seven

Girl: He's thirty-seven …

*(To **Man**)* What's your name?

Young Man: *(to **Girl**)* It's Andrew.

*(To **Man**)* Come on, you need to pull yourself up, one, two, three.

(He struggles to hold on to the man.)

Girl: Ehhh, Andrew, he said, Andrew. He's trying to get him out now …

(He pulls him out and they both fall on the grass bank.)

Girl: He's out, OK, what should we do? Alright, please hurry… *(She hangs up and backs away.)*

Man: *(breathless)* I'm sorry; I just couldn't take it any more.

Young Man: Is the ambulance coming?

Girl: Yes, they're on their way.

(We hear sirens in the distance.)

Young Man: It's all right Andrew, you're gonna be OK now.

*(He takes off his jacket and wraps it around **Andrew**.)*

Young Man: *(goes to **Girl**)* Are you OK?

Girl: Yeah, I just didn't know what to do, thank God you arrived, I couldn't hold him any longer …

Young Man: I'm Jason.

(He offers his hand, she takes it.)

Girl: Cheryl, *(whispers)* they said not to get too close in case he changes his mind and pulls us in with him.

Young Man: Christ, really?

*(He looks at **Andrew** and decides to keep his distance.)*

Hang in there, Andrew, they're nearly here …

*(They watch nervously as **Andrew** sits shivering on the grass. The sirens get louder. End.)*

Ode To Life

By Richie O'Sullivan

Frank: *A pianist, 83 years old*

Lucy: *Frank's granddaughter, 26 years old*

The stage is completely dark except for a spotlight that is lighting a man standing stage right.

Frank is dressed impeccably well in a coat tail tuxedo. He is slightly hunched over and shuffles when he walks. As the light comes up on him, he is looking out to the audience as if looking into a mirror and fixing his wispy grey hair. He ties his bow tie.

There is an excited hum from the audience in anticipation.

Stage left another spotlight appears and lights a lone black piano stool, facing downstage.

Frank slowly makes his way to the stool, to the sound of rising applause. Frank takes his seat facing the audience and the audience hushes to silence.

Frank closes his eyes and begins to mime playing a piano. There is no piano on stage but he mimes playing the piece with precision.

**The piece of music he plays is "Ode to Life" by Don Pullen - beginning at 4 minutes 27 seconds into the song.

As the music builds, his face gets more animated, feeling each beat and note as he plays.

(At 6 minutes 25 seconds into the song as the music reaches a crescendo)

Suddenly there is a crash of a bin from off stage and the sound of a startled cat. **Frank** stops playing and the music stops instantly as he looks around. The light on stage changes to a more natural lighting state.

Frank looks around his small apartment and rubs his cold arms.

Lucy, his granddaughter, appears. She is carrying a dressing gown. She walks across to Frank and wraps the dressing gown around his shoulders. She gently gives him a kiss on the head and they give each other a smile. She leaves the room.

Franks thinks for a moment while rubbing his hands, which are no longer agile but are showing signs of arthritis.

Wanting to finish his performance, **Frank** closes his eyes and he returns to the auditorium. The lights return to the spotlight on the piano.

Frank sits with his hands in his lap as the music resumes from where it left off. The emotion in his face reflects the pace and beat of the music and towards the end a tear falls down his cheek.

As the music is coming to an end he wipes the tear from his face. **Frank** stands centre stage and takes his bow, then shuffles off to bed.

Sanctuary

By Liz Quinn

A beach. The rhythmic sound of waves and cackle of seagulls. A woman is sitting with her face turned to the sun, breathing in the salty air, trousers rolled up to her calves.

Molly: *(sings softly)* My bonnie lies over the ocean, my bonnie lies over the sea, My bonnie lies over the ocean, so bring back my bonnie to me.

(Picking up momentum, Molly also picks up two pebbles and starts to clack in time with the singing.)

Bring back, O bring back, O bring back my bonnie to me, to meeee. Bring back, O bring back, O bring back my bonnie toooo meeeeeee.

(Scoops up a handful of pebbles in her hands and rattles them for 'applause'.)

Thank you, thank you ... no ... no ... you are too kind. Really. Encore? Well, I suppose, if you insist. *(Clears throat and sings passionately.)* The winds have blown over the ocean, the winds have blown over the sea, the winds have blown over the ocean, and brought back my bonnie to meee.

(*A man walks upstage carrying a picnic basket, watching* **Molly**.)

Bring back, O bring back, O bring back my bonnie to me to me. Bring back, O bring back, O bring back my bonnie to meee … aagghhh.

Dan: Very nice

Molly: Funny

Dan: No, really. You are very talented.

Molly: Do you mind?

Dan: (*sits*) Not at all.

Molly: It's rude to creep up on people. Creepy too.

Dan: I didn't mean to rudely creep. Or be creepily rude for that matter.

(*Seagulls cackle.*)

Molly: There's plenty of space on this beach.

Dan: I know.

Molly: (*to herself*) Why do I always attract the weirdos?

Dan: (*breathes deeply.*) Ahhhh. The sea air. Time for breakfast.

(**Dan** *takes out a small camping stove and lights it up. Humming* 'My bonnie lies over the ocean', *he starts to fry sausages.*)

Molly: You'll attract rats.

Dan: Well, they do say that you are never more than twenty feet from a rat.

Molly: Nice.

Dan: Oh yes. They make great pets too.

Molly: Well you're a regular David Attenborough aren't you?

Dan: Just making conversation.

Molly: I prefer the peace.

Dan: You were having quite the disco earlier.

Molly: I didn't know anyone was around.

Dan: Obviously.

Molly: I'm going.

Dan: Sorry. No, don't go. I'll mind my own business. Stay and have a sausage.

Molly: Excuse me?

Dan: Have some breakfast. Please. I brought real coffee. The fancy plunger one. Fairtrade.

Molly: It's a cafetière?

Dan: Yep, that's the one.

Molly: I don't want to have breakfast with you.

Dan: I have napkins.

Molly: I'm going to go away. Maybe London. I'll stay with Anna in Lewisham. Go shopping, see Big Ben. Drink.

Dan: Why am I being punished?

Molly: I'm not punishing you. It's best for both of us, surely you can see that. Last night was ... and we both said too much. We've both made mistakes.

Dan: You've never forgiven me.

Molly: No.

Dan: I forgave you.

Molly: You didn't.

Dan: The rat is deserting the sinking ship.

Molly: Jesus Dan, I'm so tired. I can't fight you any more.

(*Seagulls cackle.*)

Dan: You can't get good black pudding in Lewisham.

Molly: I hate black pudding. I fucking detest black pudding.

Dan: I know.

(***Molly** and **Dan** sit quietly listening to the sea surf and the sizzle of the sausages.*)

Dan: Do you remember that night we came down here? You stripped off and ran straight in. You said you were going to follow the moon.

Molly: Easily done after two bottles of wine.

Dan: More like three.

Molly: I lost my silver bracelet that night.

Dan: Have I lost you?

Molly: Your sausages are burning.

Dan: If you go, I'll do something stupid. I'll go off the rails, become an addict … heroin, most likely, to dull the pain, start stealing from little old ladies to feed my habit,

Molly: (*stands*) I'm going.

Dan: …end up in jail, doing bird, getting eyed up by heavily set tattooed men…, I'll start self-harming, slamming my head against the wall, slashing my wrists with blunt instruments, hacking …

Molly: Enough.

Dan: *(shouts)* NO! It's not enough. Don't leave. How can you be so selfish?

Molly: Enough. I'm not doing it. I can't talk or scream or cry any more. We have to let it go, let each other go. It's time now.

Dan: What will I do?

Molly: *(sits)* You'll be fine, we both will.

*(**Dan** hands **Molly** a cup.)*

Dan: There's fruit salad in the Tupperware.

Molly: Great.

Dan: *(tenderly)* I hate you.

Molly: I hate you too.

*(**Molly** and **Dan** look out and listen to the roll of the sea.)*

Blackout.

The Ramblers

By Graham Stull

*A man, **Alan**, sitting on a log, stoking a fire. Next to him, curled up in a blanket, a **Young Man** is lying on the ground.*

Young Man: Alan?

Alan: I thought you were asleep

Young Man: I can't sleep. Alan, tell me again about Ireland.

Alan: This *is* Ireland.

Young Man: No, I mean, *Ireland*. The way it was, before the Collapse.

Alan: What do you want to know?

Young Man: Well … were there many people?

Alan: Millions of them.

Young Man: And were there cars?

Alan: There were. Millions of them.

Young Man: Which were there more of? Cars or people?

Alan: *(thinking)* I couldn't say. Maybe equal numbers of both.

Young Man: What colour were the cars?

Alan: All colours. Now, enough, go to sleep. We've a long ways to go tomorrow.

(Brief silence.)

Young Man: Alan?

Alan: What?

Young Man: Wit' all them people, was there enough for everyone to eat? Or did some go hungry? Or did they have to eat rats?

Alan: No one et' rats. We all had lovelier things than rats to eat.

Young Man: What things? Magpies? Hares?

Alan: *(smiling at the memory)* Cheeseburgers.

Young Man: What's that?

Alan: I couldn't explain. Just imagine something lovelier than rat and magpie *and* blackberries.

Young Man: Lovelier than hare?

Alan: As well.

(Brief silence.)

Young Man: Alan?

Alan: Will you ever just go to sleep?

Young Man: It must have been wonderful in Ireland. With their colourful cars and their cheeburs ... I'd say all them people were very happy back then. Weren't they just, Alan?

Alan: *(reflecting)* No happier than us is now, I suppose.

Young Man: Why not?

Alan: I couldn't say. I was younger than you at the time. But … me ma and da were always fightin', so they were. Bickerin'.

Young Man: What about?

Alan: Different things. *(Reminiscing)* I remember Da lost his job, just before the Collapse happened, that was. Ma gave out awful stink to him about that. She said she was gonna leave him. But she never did.

Young Man: What's a "job"?

Alan: Something people did back then. Instead of hunting rats.

Young Man: So did they hunt for cheeburs?

Alan: I don't remember. They looked at tellies, I think. You know, them little picture boxes I told you about t'other day.

Young Man: Yeah … I wish we had a telly, Alan. I sorely would like to see one of them tellies, I would.

Alan: Maybe we'll find a telly when we get to the Strand.

(Brief pause.)

Young Man: Alan?

Alan: What is it now?

Young Man: Did people have friends in Ireland? Like the way you and me is friends?

Alan: I don't think so. Not like you and me.

Young Man: But if there was millions of people, they must've found it right easy to make friends?

Alan: That's not how it works. The more people there is, the less they talk to each other. When there's millions, no one talks to anyone at all.

Young Man: What did people do if they didn't talk to each other?

Alan: They looked at the tellies. They went to their jobs. And they drove their cars.

(Brief pause.)

Young Man: Alan?

Alan: What?

Young Man: I don't think I would have liked Ireland, after all. Not if you wasn't my friend, I wouldn't like it. Not even if I had a telly and a whole load of cheeburs to eat.

Alan: Good. 'Cause anyway we can't go back in the past. Now, *for the last time*, just go to sleep.

*(**Alan** lies down and covers himself with a blanket.)*

Young Man: Good night, Alan. I love you.

Alan: I love you too, boy.

*(**Alan** reaches out and they hold hands, before turning to fall asleep. The flames burn down and fade to black.)*

Soul Mates

By Maeve Binchy

In the waiting room of an Opticians. Two patients, waiting for their appointments.

Rose, nurse, late twenties, great reader of books who thinks reluctantly that print is getting smaller and that she needs reading glasses.

Kevin, teacher, early thirties, much mocked in his school for his owlish appearance, needs cool frames.

It is entirely interior monologues but they DO acknowledge each other with nods and glances across the magazine table.

Rose: You know, they really know what they're doing in this place, there's NO lighting here at all, anyone would think they were going blind. I never thought my eyes would go. I always thought it would be the legs, that I'd get ropes of veins like my mam, but no, they're fine, they'd take me anywhere. It's the eyes that died on me.

Kevin: I suppose he'll say I'm a fool to want something trendy. I don't even know what trendy is. But other guys wear glasses and the kids don't say Too Whit Too Woo when they come into the classroom.

Rose: I had no idea how dark it was in here, I can't finish the new Colm Toibin, there's no point in my picking up one of those glossy magazines, I'd only see the pictures.

Kevin: That woman across the room has the new Colm Toibin beside her, never opened it, not once. Probably bought it to show off anyway. God, women are beyond belief. I mean, I thought I understood Hilary. And now it's all solicitors' fees the whole time and threats of palimony and demands for support. I mean, she lived in MY house and when it was over it was over. If it was HER house, I'd have gone. It was never OUR house.

Rose: I suppose it won't matter having glasses. Nobody sees me when I'm reading. Charlie just HATED when I got lost in a book. I remember trying to tell him the story of My Cousin Rachel, and he didn't even care whether Rachel was a heroine or a villain. 'It's only an old story,' he kept saying.

But there won't be any more fellows in the near future, the flat's too small for one thing. Charlie and I were always falling over each other. Anyway, I'm too tired when I get off my shift in the hospital, all I need is a good bath, something to put in the microwave and my book.

Kevin: I wonder what Hilary would advise about glasses. She was always interested in how I looked, I'll give her that. At the start, we were great pals, it's lonely without her. I tell the lads that I'm playing the field, but I'm not really. I just go home after school, correct the essays, set up classes for the next day, read a bit, look at television. The house seems very big for me, but there you go.

Rose: Charlie left shrugging his shoulders, carrying all his belongings in one bag. No fuss, no rows. Only mystification that I actually LIKED reading things that never happened, old stories, old made-up things.

Kevin: God that girl across the waiting room must be learning the pattern on the carpet off by heart. Hasn't she a book beside her and a stack of magazines on the table. Of course, she could be going blind or something. She has a kind sort of face.

Rose: That fellow with the Billy Bunter glasses over there has a nice face, bet he's a vet or something kind. Of course those kind faces often turn out to be desperate things like bankers. Or dropouts like Charlie who don't believe in taxes, or working all day, or anything like that.

Kevin: I could talk to her but … I mustn't do that. Not any more.

Rose: I could ask him if he comes here often. Or something a bit less silly. But then he mightn't want to talk, he's been reading that soccer gossip magazine since I came in. He's content the way he is, he doesn't want to be bothered. I'm so used to starting conversations because I do that all day in the hospital. I should be glad of a bit of peace here and I would be glad, if only I could read.

Kevin: I only wish I had asked her for a loan of that book. SHE wasn't reading it, I'd be well stuck into it now rather than this stupid magazine about soccer players and their wives.

It could have been a peaceful half an hour. But then the risk, the sheer risk … At least I've learned not to do that any more.

Oh yes, he's ready for me, good.

(Kevin smiles at Rose).

*(To **Rose**)* I won't be long in there, just choosing new frames actually.

Rose: The ones you have are fine.

Kevin: *(to himself)* That's funny. No one ever said that before.

She'd be really bad news. Just sitting there fidgeting and looking uneasy. Why HAVE a book if you're not going to read it. I couldn't take another three years of that, even if she WERE interested.

*(To **Rose**)* Good luck now.

Rose: Pity he's really up himself about the bloody frames. Nothing wrong with his glasses. I wouldn't want to be within a mile of him, him and his football and the Wags and the whole culture. Let him go. No, Rose, no more smiling at him or the likes of him. Soon I'll have nice big glass eyes and can read properly. That's what I will do, until I fall over a soul mate somewhere along the line.

Head down now, no more eye contact. Okay, breathe again.

Hearts

By Lucy Montague-Moffatt

Characters:

Old woman 1

Old woman 2

Location:

Putting out the washing.

Old Woman 1: How's the knitting coming?

Old Woman 2: Great, yesterday I knitted a young man.

Old Woman 1: Oh that's just lovely.

Old Woman 2: Yes, he has blue hair and purple eyebrows and is full of love.

Old Woman 1: How is he full of love?

Old Woman 2: I knitted 1,000 little red hearts inside him before I sewed him up.

Old Woman 1: Must have taken you hours.

Old Woman 2: Two episodes of *Winning Streak* and one *Late Late Show*.

Old Woman 1: What does your Tony think?

Old Woman 2: He's very jealous. He did the washing up all last week.

Old Woman 1: He loves you really.

Old Woman 2: I know, I know, but he only has one heart.

Old Woman 1: He's got two arms.

Old Woman 2: And two legs, but what good is that to me?

Old Woman 1: Just don't get carried away.

Old Woman 2: I'm already floating.

Old Woman 1: Last week I knitted some gloves, if you'd like to bring them to Tony for me.

Old Woman 2: Why?

Old Woman 1: His hands must be broken from all that washing up.

Old Woman 2: I'm sure he wouldn't like anything like that; he's a very simple man.

Old Woman 1: Oh that's a pity.

Old Woman 2: The knitting has gotten too much for him.

Old Woman 1: How so?

Old Woman 2: Late last night, I tried to open him up and knit some hearts into him.

Old Woman 1: Bet he didn't like that.

Old Woman 2: He told me that I'd broken his heart.

Old Woman 1: That's the trouble with only having one.

Old Woman 2: If he had more maybe he wouldn't be so sad.

Old Woman 1: I've never seen him look sad.

Old Woman 2: Ah he's always sad these days, I'm sick of it.

Old Woman 1: Sometimes he waves to me, over the back wall. Most days.

Old Woman 2: He's a simple man.

Old Woman 1: Well at least you have your young lad, with the blue hair.

Old Woman 2: That's something, thank God.

Old Woman 1: Well, I better be off.

Old Woman 2: Where are you rushing off to?

Old Woman 1: Going to go knit some hearts into my gloves.

Old Woman 2: Aw, that'll be nice.

The End

The Straight Talk

By Keith Farnan

A young man is standing behind a bank counter with a computer and phone next to him. He is dressed in a white shirt and blue tie. Posters on the wall promise lower interest rates and one reads "Come in for a chat, sure, it's only (your) money!"

A middle-aged man arrives at the counter, hands a slip of paper across the counter. He looks dishevelled and wild eyed.

Teller: Hi there, can I help you?

Customer: Yes, I'd like to take my money out of my account.

Teller: Certainly ... and how much would you like?

Customer: All of it.

Teller: I'm sorry, all of it did you say?

Customer: Yes, all of it. *(**Teller** looks at slip and types on keyboard.)*

Teller: But I've just checked your account. You have quite a lot of money.

Customer: Yes.

Teller: And no debts to speak of ...

Customer: That's right. *(impatiently)*

Teller: Well, this is a most unusual situation. You see, most people, well, most people in your situation, of your age. They just don't leave. We have our hooks pretty deep into them by then, so they can't leave.

Customer: I don't care.

Teller: Well Sir, this is quite unprecedented. I can't help you. I'm not authorised. Let me just call my supervisor.

*(The **Teller** gets on his phone while the **Customer** starts to tap the counter.)*

Teller: Sir, could you come down? Yes. It's a code one.

Customer: I don't understand. I simply want my money. You are the teller. That's the slip. Here's my ID *(takes ID out of his pocket and slams it on the counter.)*

Teller: The manager is coming right down. If I could ask you to bear with my passivity and fear of individual action for just a few moments.

*(The **Manager**, a well-groomed, bespectacled man, strides in and shakes the hand of the **Customer**. He speaks with an unerring cheerfulness, regardless of the **Customer's** responses.)*

Manager: So good to see you again.

Customer: We've never met.

Manager: How's the wife?

Customer: She's dead.

Manager: How are the kids?

Customer: They emigrated.

Manager: How's the dog?

Customer: He emigrated as well.

Manager: Pleasantries concluded, unpleasantries imminent. We don't have your money.

Customer: What?

Manager: We. Don't. Have. Your. Money. We never really had it. As soon as it was on the system, we used it as leverage to buy government bonds of some unknown country and we can't recover it. That country's disappeared. We won't recover anything. Truthfully, we never really had any money, we simply had trust. *(Bombastically)* And confidence, God, we had confidence. But, let's be fair you never really had anything of any value. You see, people don't understand. Those dirty little pieces of papers, or money as you call it, are simply promises that someone somewhere assures you is worth something. I mean, did you think the ink was valuable? When was the last time you believed a promise just because it's written down. Don't be naive. Go home. Relax. We're the bank who cares.

Customer: *(helplessly)* You, you can't do this, this is outrageous.

Manager: Yes. Yes it is. Yes we can. In fact, we already have. I have gentle platitudes which might avoid a scene if you'd like but you don't need them, you're going to shake your head in defeat and walk away.

*(**Customer** looks at them both, angry but powerless, tries not to walk away. Eventually, shakes his head and walks away. Once out of sight, the **Manager** turns to the **Teller** and high fives him as he strides away.)*

Knowing

By Geraldine McAlinden

Dedicated to my mum, Ita Rose McAlinden (1936 to 2010)

Lights up.

Woman *sits at a table, with a mug.*

Woman: You know when you're in the hospital, and your mother and father are on the ward while you're in a side office, with the doctor and your brothers and sisters, and the doctor's telling you that your mother has between one and two months? And one of your brothers and all of your sisters are crying? And he tells you that, no, you shouldn't tell your mother, because the shock might kill her? And you ask the doctor about the switch, and he looks at you. So you tell him about the switch that the G.P. told your mother about, the one that can turn off the cancer, the miracle switch that she's going to find? And the doctor looks at you and says no, it's not a good idea to tell her, she only has between one and two months to find it? And you check the date on the paper and start to count the days ... 30 days has September ... so does that mean a thirty-day month or a thirty-one-day month?

And you know the way that when you're doing the shopping, you have to find the food with the furthest best before date because that means that your mother won't die before then? But you wonder if that packet of bacon will outlive her?

And you buy new mugs, nice, Belleek, small, otherwise the visitors'll stay all night. And the doctor said she only has a certain amount of energy so you have to save some of it? And your aunt bursts into tears in the kitchen while one of the neighbours snipes that your ma's looking awful well and how long has she now? And her friend takes umbrage when you give her the bum's rush and stays away till your sister-in-law has to ring her to invite her back up again?

And you know the way your mother wants to get to the bathroom on her zimmer before the carers come, because she doesn't want them poking about her? So you're trying to balance her at the same time as getting your father his insulin, and you drop her and she smashes against the bath guard, cracking it, and you wonder have you broke her? And she tells you not to tell the district nurse.

And you know the way you try to warn your father what's ahead and he shouts at you, the only time he's got angry, that we won't get a miracle unless we really believe?

And you know the way that you start to hate the ticking of a clock, so you take out all the batteries but you can't stop your heart pulsing in your ears? And you go to work for the distraction, because your head is going to explode if you stay at home. But you catch people looking at you, and you know they're thinking how the fuck can you be so heartless? And they're easier to face than the kind ones.

And you know when you balance on the armchair that the Macmillan nurse brought, to get a photo with your mummy, the last one, and she leans over and carefully sweeps the hair out of your eyes, and tucks it behind your left ear and tells you that you're the best child in Ireland? And then she asks you, what was it that doctor wanted to talk to you all about ...

(Lights fade.)

Blisters

By Patrick O'Sullivan

Man *in his thirties or forties*

Older Man *in his sixties or seventies*

Scene: Summer. Countryside. There is a large rock. A log lies across a stream.

The two men enter the scene. They are hiking. Both carry rucksacks on their backs. Both have a set of walking sticks.

Older Man: Let's stop here; I need to change my socks.

Man: Are your feet at you?

Older Man: Yeah.

*(**Older Man** puts down his walking sticks by the large rock and takes off his rucksack, laying it gently beside his sticks. He sits down slowly on the rock. He begins to untie his bootlaces.*

***Man** stands, looking around. Eventually he sits down on the log that traverses the stream.*

***Older Man** takes off his boot. He places it beside him, carefully. He then takes off his sock and examines the sole of his foot. He* *places the sock onto a small rock beside him. He then repeats the actions with the other boot and sock.)*

Man: Blisters?

Older Man: Yeah, one there and one on the way.

Man: Oh no. Have you anything with you?

Older Man: Like what?

Man: Like those blister plasters.

Older Man: No, I used my last one yesterday.

Man: Ah Dad, how many times have I told you?

Older Man: I have this though. (***Older Man** takes a hip flask out of the pocket of his jacket.)* An oul drop of the creatur!

Man: What are you going to do with that, rub it on your feet?

*(**Older Man** laughs. **Man** is smiling.)*

*(**Older Man** takes a swig out of the flask.)*

Older Man: Here. *(Passing the flask to the **Man**).*

Man: Thanks.

*(**Man** takes a drink from the flask and hands it back to the **Older Man**.)*

This is our third year at this.

Older Man: What?

Man: Dublin to Dursey ... our epic trek.

Older Man: Oh. Yeah. So it is.

Man: We're more than halfway there now.

Older Man: That'd be about right.

Man: The best week of the year is this holiday.

Older Man: Don't let your mother hear you say that!

Man: She's invited every year, Dad, and she always says no.

Older Man: Ah, you know what she's like.

Man: Mars or Snickers?

Older Man: Mars.

*(**Man** throws a Mars Bar to **Older Man,** who catches it.)*

Older Man: There's no talking to her.

Man: Why, have you tried?

Older Man: What do you mean?

Man: Mam. You. Everything that's been going on.

Older Man: Don't be so smart!

Man: I'm just saying …

Older Man: Well don't.

*(**Older Man** opens the wrapper of the bar and starts to eat it. **Man** takes off one of his boots and sock and examines his ankle.)*

Older Man: How's the heel?

Man: A lot better.

Older Man: Good.

Man: I think the bath did it good.

Older Man: Have another one tonight.

Man: I will. Followed by a slow-cooked leg of lamb.

Older Man: We're blessed with the girls. Roast beef, legs of lamb, apple tarts.

Man: Spoiled rotten we are.

Older Man: You're a lucky man.

Man: I am.

Older Man: You don't know how lucky.

Man: I do, Dad.

(Pause.)

Are you ready to go on?

Older Man: Yeah. *(Stays sitting, staring into space)*

I should have done this years ago.

Man: Hiking?

Older Man: Yeah. With you. With all of you.

Man: Well we're doing it now Dad. Not too many fathers and sons have walked across Ireland together.

Older Man: I know.

Man: You OK?

Older Man: I feel a bit cold.

Man: Come on and we'll get going; you'll soon warm up when we're walking.

Older Man: *(not moving)* You're right, son. You're right.

Thorny Island

By Sarah Binchy

Deck of a ferry ship. A curved railing. Seagulls, projection of sky, sea.

Girl, *mid-20s, duffle coat, jeans, small rucksack, leans on rail.*

Boy, *same age, suit, laptop, approaches, hands her a takeaway cup of tea.*

Girl *sips tea.*

Boy *watches her.*

Boy: I suppose you don't want me to get you some food ...

   Like a sausage roll or something ...

*(**Girl** winces and grips the rail.)*

Boy: Sorry.

(He tentatively puts his arm around her, falters, turns it into a pat.)

(She points out to sea.)

Girl: That's where I'd like to be right now.

Boy: I've been there. There's a boat that goes out from Coliemore Harbour.

We should go there together. For a picnic. It'll be fun.

(*Checks for a reaction.*)

Or I'll row you out and leave you there if you prefer.

(*Hint of a smile from her.*)

(**Boy** *takes her arm, points.*)

See the stripy towers? See that tall building? Now move over to the right. Bit more.

Girl: That big glass thing?

Boy: No, the short ugly building squatting beside it. That's my office.

Girl: How'd you get off work today anyway?

Boy: I phoned my boss, I said, "You know how I never call in sick? Well this morning I must call in sick."

See, I didn't actually lie.

I'm glad you asked me. Even if it was last minute.

(*Pause.*)

Girl: Well I've told people I'm off to an intensive yoga workshop in Sussex.

I don't even know where Sussex is.

Boy: And you appear to have forgotten your yoga mat.

(**Girl** *laughs then stops herself.*)

Girl: I should've flown. This just prolongs it.

Boy: I told you I would've paid the air fare.

Girl: It feels like a daytrip, like we're meant to be having fun. It's not fun. It's shit.

Boy: I know.

Girl: You don't know. You're saying, let's have picnics, like, really?

Do you see us even wanting to see each other after this?

We hardly even know each other.

Boy: *(quiet)* Well I would. I like you. But whatever you want is OK.

Girl: Whatever I want, that's what you keep saying. Why don't you have an opinion?

Boy: I voiced my opinion.

Girl: Was that an opinion? "Whatever you want to do is cool with me." You call that an opinion?

Boy: I didn't say "cool".

Girl: You didn't say "Stop".

Boy: I said I'll support you.

Girl: But you left the decision up to me.

Boy: But it has to be your decision, it's your body.

Girl: See that's just a cop-out. It's my body but it's our mess.

I know how this is going to go.

You know, it's going to be a drag between us after this. You'll feel guilty and call me from time to time. But it'll gradually fizzle away. It certainly won't be "fun". And you'll say to yourself, well that's a pity but I did the right thing all along. I was a great guy.

Boy: Well if you're going to completely misrepresent me –

Girl: Then tell me not to do it. Make a decision.

Boy: *(brightening)* You've changed your mind?

Girl: I haven't made up my mind.

I'm here because I couldn't figure out what else to do.

Mean it when you say you'll support me. Be in my life. Make this not be a disaster.

(She watches him.)

Boy: Can I think about it?

Girl: Until we get to Holyhead.

(She takes his hand. He does not respond at first, then pushes his and her hands into her coat pocket.

Both gaze out to sea.)

Voices In The Tunnel

By Garrett Keogh

John, *suit and tie, sits on a wooden bench in a corridor, his head in his hands.*

Footsteps echo on the high walls and stone floors, indistinct conversations rise and fall – people somewhere off hurrying by, coming and going.

Laura, *dark-suited, high heels, enters.*

John: Oh.

Laura: *(looking back the way she came)* It's eh … Eh …

John: Busy?

(She sighs.)

(He shifts along the bench.)

John: Do you want to …?

Laura: Eh …

John: It's ok. It's not…

Laura: What?

John: Against the rules?

(She sits down. A little apart. Noises off as before.)

Laura: I didn't expect to …

John: No, there's no room. They're in corridors. And out the door …

Laura: I don't know what I imagined.

(Pause.)

John: It won't take long.

Laura: No …

(He looks at watch.)

John: But they're running late. He said. You gave me that. *(watch)*

(She stands.)

Laura: John…!

John: Sorry.

(He stands.)

John: Please. Laura … Please sit down. I've told him, full disclosure. Everything, whatever she wants, I said.

(She sits. Footsteps, etc., as before.)

John: This place gives me the willies. The walls, the floors, they're cold, they're damp. And those … The people who work here, coming and going … They're not, they're not like … They're not real people. Hear them? Self-important, busy, they move, they carry, they *huddle* …! Do they have someone polish their shoes?

Laura: What?

John: Clack-clack, clack-clack … To make them make that sound? Folders, files, polished shoes and gowns … There's a fortune to be made in misery.

Laura: Sit down.

John: Dealing, wheeling, whispering. And the real people, the, the … Us, all the us's, queuing round the block? We don't exist. No, not in the world according to them.

Laura: John.

John: They make the rules in this tennis game.

Laura: Sit. Down.

(He sits.)

John: Click-clack, click-clack …

Laura: Stop. Stop it.

John: Stone cold echoes in a tunnel.

Laura: I'll go.

John: You already have.

(She sighs. Footsteps. Voices, off, but nearer now. They look up in anticipation.)

John: Is this us …?

(Sounds subside. He looks at his watch.)

John: This saved us once.

Laura: What?

John: Remember in the cave …? In Spain? Like this, cold, damp, echoey …? But the air there was dry. And full of promise. And my watch, the watch you gave me, saved the day.

Laura: No.

John: Yes. It was the only thing that made us see in the dark when we got lost. Like children playing with a torch, remember?

Laura: No. We didn't get lost. You left the path. You stopped to look at something.

John: A stalactite.

Laura: And the guide moved on. The lights in that cavern went out. It was pitch black.

John: Except for the dial on the watch.

Laura: And their voices, fading off down the tunnel …

John: It was a laugh.

Laura: Was it? Going along bowed to the ground … In case we'd fall. Miss the step. Go into the bloody lake!

John: We laughed.

Laura: Hundreds of feet underground … Stuck, with someone who wants to play like a child …?

John: It was heart in the mouth for a minute, but … We laughed. And we got out.

(Footsteps, voices, echo off.)

(She stands.)

Laura: I think this is them now.

(He stands.)

John: We got out. Laura …

Laura: I don't like caves, John. The dark. I never did.

(He hands her the watch.)

John: Here. Here …! You have everything else.

Laura: *(refusing to take it)* I know where I'm going.

(She goes. Her high heels click-clack across the stone floor. The lights fade and the noises off rise to a sickening twisted crescendo: the clatter of heels. The indistinct chatter. He sinks to his knees. And the echoing darkness envelops him. Suddenly the watch gives out a strange thin beam of light. Stronger than the glow of an L.E.D. More surreal than a torch. He crawls off following this thread of light. The noises reduce to a drip-drip deep in a cave underground.

Blackout.)

Weekend Abroad

By Federico Storni

*At the centre of the stage there is a table with two chairs ready for a breakfast for two. At the centre of the table there is a fondue kit, which is decorated with a Swiss flag. **HE** is sitting on the sofa in a morning dress decorated with a Swiss motif, and is surfing on the Internet through his laptop, which is covered with a "Swiss flag skin" (the internet sites that he will open may or may not be screened on stage during the conversation). **SHE** is on the other side of the table (in a sort of kitchen), slicing Emmental with a comically big Swiss army knife. **SHE** is also wearing a morning dress that matches the one that **HE** is wearing.*

HE: Wow!

SHE: *(wincing)* What? What happened?

HE: Let's fly to Ireland this weekend! There's a wonderful offer: round trip from Zurich to either Dublin or Belfast for only 1 franc!

SHE: *(doubtful)* Gee, I don't know … I don't really know nothing about Ireland. Aren't they all violent drunkards? Isn't there a war going on? And, also, aren't they, like, two different nations?

HE: No idea. Until two minutes ago I thought that Dublin and Belfast were two different names for the same city. However, when in *The Simpsons* and in *Family Guy* they go to or have relations with Ireland or Irish people it's always fun to watch. Also in *How I Met Your Mother*. You know, St Patrick's day and shit. Let me check.

SHE: I think they are different nations ...

HE: Yes, probably. They have two different national football teams. *(Perplexed)* But only one rugby team. What ...? *(Pauses)* Nope. St Patrick's Day isn't next week.

SHE: So, in which nation should we go?

HE: No idea. They seem the same to me. Wait. Do you remember in what city U2's "Sunday Bloody Sunday" was set? Never mind, I'll search it.

SHE: In any case, we should rule out the nation the song is about and choose the other one. It seems safer.

HE: Then ... wait ... Ireland and Belfast it is!

SHE: Yeah, I'm still not sure. I still think Irishmen are violent and drunkards as a rule. Every time there's an Irishman in a TV series, there's also a fight ... Also, do they have, like, a culture? Something to visit?

HE: Probably. Here it says that this year there's something called *The Gathering Ireland*, which is *(quotation mark gesture)* "a spectacular, year-long celebration of all things Irish".

SHE: Yeah ... that doesn't help much ...

HE: Yeah ... Also, some think this event is somehow disrespectful of the Irish diaspora.

SHE: They had a diaspora? How cultural! When?

*(In the audience, in the front row, there will be seated from the beginning of the play a **LEPRECHAUN**: red haired, green dressed, with a pipe.)*

LEPRECHAUN: *(standing up, with a strong Irish accent)* Fuck it! Fuck you! This is bollocks. You don't know nothing about Ireland. This is racism, not theatre!

*(**HE** and **SHE** break off character; they take their morning dresses off. Under them, they are normally dressed. They also start speaking with a marked Irish accent.)*

HE: That's exactly the point.

LEPRECHAUN: How could this be the point? You are Irishmen, for God's sake, you should know better! What's the point in dressing up as some typical Swiss dudes and then delivering racial stereotypes?

HE: *(under his breath)* ...says the *leprechaun*...

LEPRECHAUN: What was that...? *Yes*, I'm dressed as a leprechaun *because* I'm embracing my culture, *not* because I'm mocking it! Can't a fellow Irishman dress up as a beloved folk character if it pleases him so?

HE: Yes! But don't you think this is also a bit stereot—

SHE: Sir, Sir! If you permit me to evaluate the author's work, I think he was trying to show how even stereotypes aren't such a bad thing, as long as they are an instrument that permits one to discover new things. For instance, I don't believe Swiss citizens usually dress like this.

AUDIENCE VOICE OFF: *(with a strong German accent) Ja*! This in *unglaublich* offensive!

SHE: Thanks ...? *(to LEPRECHAUN)* If you hadn't inter-rupted the play, you would have seen how we would have changed our preconceptions about Ireland and Irish peo-ple with just a bit of information.

LEPRECHAUN: *(sceptical)* All this in only four minutes? ... Go on, I'm curious.

VOICE OFF-STAGE: Sorry, the time is up.

HE, SHE, and LEPRECHAUN: Fuck!

(They all leave the scene in an angry way.)

Isolation

By Joan Ryan

Going up

                           Stand clear of the doors

Leave a message

                                 going down

Mind the gap

                          You have two old messages

Turn right

                         you have one new message

Going down

                              change here for …

Leave a message

                                                    Top up

5th floor

                                        please leave the building

Top up

                                                stand clear

Leave a message

                                                    going up

Mind the gap

                                                turn around

You are out of credit

                                                    turn left

Leave a message

                                                going down

Next stop

                                        please go to checkout

Now

                                                stand clear

Isolation – Joan Ryan

Going

next stop

Going

down

You have four euro and ten cent credit

you have no new messages

store closes in five minutes

mind the gap

you have two old messages

please go to checkout immediately

going down

stand clear

fourth floor

top up

we are approaching a pocket of turbulence

going down

leave a message

please go to checkout now

Leave a message

going down

Tiny Plays For Ireland

Do not leave your seats until the seatbelt sign says so

Stand clear

                                                 go to checkout

Leave a message

                          I'm not here to take your call right now

Next stop

                                      You have no messages

Please top up

                                         Mind the gap

Stand clear

                                              Going

Down

I'm not here to take your call right now

                                          Leave a message

The Phone Records

by Kevin Gildea

*There are two characters: a **Man** and a **Woman**.*

*The **Man** is in a hotel bed, away on business.*

*The **Woman** is at home.*

We see only the man.

Before, between and after calls there is darkness.

He is asleep each time the phone rings.

When the phone rings he switches a bedside lamp on and is in a hotel bed. We only ever see the upper part of the bed – his torso and head only are visible in a sea of dark. When he switches the lamp off there is complete darkness.

Call 1

*(Phone rings. **Man** picks up the receiver.)*

Woman: Hello. Hello? Hello!?

Man: Uh – hello.

(**Man** *turns on the light.*)

Woman: Are you okay?

Man: I was sleeping. It's late here.

Woman: You were working late again?

Man: Yeah – this thing has taken on a life of its own so ... I've had to reschedule.

Woman: So ... you won't be back tomorrow

(*There is silence.*)

Man: How are the kids?

Woman: Tom's got a temperature and Amy ... is Amy. She made a card for you – with a heart.

Man: Nice.

Woman: I put it with the others.

Man: Great ...

(*Silence.*)

Man: I better go.

Woman: Okay.

(**Man** *replaces receiver and turns off light.*)

Call 2

(*Phone rings.* **Man** *turns on light.* **Man** *picks up phone.*)

Woman: Jim? Jim!

Man: Uh ... hello.

Woman: It's Tom – his temperature is 40 and …

Man: I'm sure it's nothing. Just get a cold cloth and …

Woman: He's vomiting.

Man: … and a bucket … I mean – a basin. I'll be home Friday.

Woman: Friday – I thought you said Thursday?

Man: We had to move Wednesday to Thursday.

(Silence.)

Woman: Goodbye.

*(**Woman** hangs up phone.)*

Man: Hello?

*(To darkness without **Man** turning off light.)*

Call 3

*(Phone rings. **Man** puts on bedside light.)*

Man: Uh … what time is it?

Woman: Tom's in hospital.

Man: Wha'?

Woman: Your son … he's in hospital.

Man: Wow.

Woman: He asked for you.

Man: Tell him I said 'Hello!' I mean – send him my love.
    Listen –

Woman: You are coming home tomorrow.

Man: The client feels

Woman: The client 'feels'! What about your son?

Man: I'm doing this for my son, for you. for all of us.

*(**Woman** hangs up. To dark.)*

Call 4

*(Phone rings. **Man** answers.)*

Woman: Jim ! Jim!

*(**Man** turns on light.)*

Man: What's wrong?

Woman: Tom's dying.

Man: Okay ... calm down ... take a deep breath

Woman: T-O-M I-S DYING!

Man: There's no need to shout.

Woman: YOUR SON IS FUCKING DYING!

Man: Do you have to curse?

Woman: Did you hear what I said?

Man: Yes I heard.

Woman: Well?

Man: That's ... sad.

Woman: Sad?!

Man: *Very* sad ... damn sad. It's DAMN sad!!

Woman: You've got to fly home tomorrow.

Man: I can't – we're *this* close.

Woman: YOUR SON IS DYING!!!

Man: Yes but I can't – I – I mean maybe, but – some people look like they're going to die but it's just ... the way things look and then they don't and everything's fine and we all look back on it and think, 'What was all that about?' ... nothing ... nothing at all ... in fact we won't even look back on it – or think about it – because it's ... nothing and nobody looks back on nothing ... so...

Woman: I don't think you appreciate what I'm saying: Your son is dying.

Man: I don't think *you* appreciate *my* position –

*(The **Woman** hangs up. **Man** switches off light.)*

Call 5.

*(Lights up. **Man** is on phone.)*

Man: Hey, it's me.

(Silence.)

Man: I've been ringing. Where have you been?

Woman: Tom's dead.

Man: I'm coming home tomorrow.

Woman: Your son is dead.

Man: When I get home I'll make it up to him.

Woman: He's dead.

Man: We'll go to his favourite restaurant – I'll buy him a meal, that'll make him happy

(Silence. Five seconds.)

Woman: Your son is dead.

Man: Let's just pack up – we'll go travelling ... for as long as you like – just the four of us.

Woman: He's dead!!!! DEAD! DEAD! DEAD! DEAD!

(She cries uncontrollably.)

Man: Okay, just the three of us then – or the two of us or ... however many of us are left. Whatever that number is – we'll go away together, *that* number of us – all together.

Hello ... hello? ... hello?

(Fade to darkness.)

Man: Hello? Hello? Hello?

Ground Meat

By Conor Hanratty

Two men. One older, both well-groomed. Both have iPhones. They're at a restaurant, eating their main courses. First date. They eat quietly before the older of the two restarts the conversation.

Paul: You probably won't believe me, but you're the first person I met like this.

David: Seriously?

Paul: Seriously.

David: You're not. For me, like.

Paul: I didn't think so, Derek. You're very cute, so I imagine you can pick and choose.

David: Ah yeah. Most people just want to have sex, like.

Paul: Don't you?

David: Sure. But like, I mean, most guys on it just don't even say hi. It's all very blunt. They wanna see the goods, and then send you their GPS location. Like they're ordering a pizza from their iPhone.

Paul: I could make a comment about pepperoni but it might be in bad taste.

David: And I've heard it before, Colm.

Paul: Sorry.

David: Like I said, you're not the first.

(They eat.)

David: So what made you want to talk to me?

Paul: (*speaking with his mouth full*) You used full sentences in your profile. And you didn't have a shirtless picture.

David: I beg your pardon?

Paul: (*finished eating*) Sorry. I said that you used full sentences in your profile.

David: I see. I read on one guy's profile that it's the apostrophe that separates us from the animals.

(Paul *finds this funnier than necessary.* **David** *is slightly uncomfortable. They eat.)*

Paul: I wonder why it's called Grindr.

David: Maybe there was already an app called "Location-based GPS Gay Hookups."

Paul: Maybe.

David: It's addictive though. I found three guys on my road who used to bully me in school. One of them has a naked photo of himself and a tagline that says, "Breed me". Totally foul, like.

Paul: I don't even know what that means.

David: Think about it.

Paul: Oh … really?

David: That's what it says. Real sexy.

Paul: Certainly.

(The conversation dwindles again.)

Paul: So what do you hope to find?

David: Oh, the usual. Beautiful husband – or even fucking civil partner, since that's all we're allowed – with good job, good body and good mental health. Hung a bonus, but not a deal-breaker.

Paul: Specific.

David: Is it? I woulda said that was the cliché. Specifically I want a six-foot-two Japanese-American cellist called Orlando who moonlights as a macrobiotic chef. That's *specific.*

Paul: I'm sure he's out there.

David: How about you? Please don't tell me you're only on it to perve on the torsos and see who's actually gay.

Paul: No. Well, not only that haha. (*David doesn't laugh*). I read about it somewhere online and I was curious, so I downloaded it to my phone. Is that what you say? Downloaded?

David: Installed.

Paul: Right. Installed. And I said hello to a few people. There's an awful lot of ugly queers around.

David: Beautiful inside. (*he winks*)

Paul: Dublin's probably too small for it though. Nothing to stop some maniac from *installing* it and then using it to track, or meet, or kill cute young gay men.

David: If you're one of them I'm definitely not going to sleep with you.

Paul: I'm not. But you get my point.

David: Sure. But maybe I'm a vigilante thug who gets a kick out of seducing and then beating up lonely old fags who failed at life and should know better.

Paul: If you're one of them I'm not paying for dinner.

David: Deal.

Paul: Fancy dessert?

David: Just a coffee. Espresso.

Paul: (*realising*) Nice.

David: By the way my name is actually David.

Paul: Paul. Nice to meet you.

(The End.)

The Night Feed

By Justine Mitchell

Late evening.

*A **Woman**, thirties, homeless, sits on a Dublin city street – begging. She is seriously strung out. A **Man** walks towards her, stops and stares.*

She notices him and eyeballs him back. This standoff lasts at least 10 seconds.

Woman: What do you want?

(He approaches her.)

Woman: Oh no.

(She makes a move to go. He blocks her. Looming over her.)

Man: Don't make a scene –

Woman: I don't want to –

Man: I only –

Woman: Help! Rape!

(He looks around him, then crouches, pins her down and puts his hand over her mouth.

A voice off, male, drunk – "Rape! Ha ha!"

Several voices off laugh in response. Mocking.

Same male voice as before – "I'll give you a raping.")

Man: I'm not going to make you do anything you don't want to.

*(The **Woman** wriggles under the man's grip.)*

Man: I'm not going to force you ... Okay?

(She considers this. She stops wriggling. And nods.

He lets her go. They are both exhausted. They pant in exhaustion.

Pause.

Finally.)

Man: Have you been using?

*(The **Woman** regards him.)*

Woman: You look old.

*(The **Man** gently takes her arm, looking at the track marks scarring it.)*

Man: Seventy last birthday.

Woman: You're seventy.

Man: Yes.

Woman: Seventy. Jesus.

(She gingerly withdraws her arm.)

Man: You haven't been here in a while.

Woman: You been watching me?

Man: I like to. Yes.

Woman: You shouldn't do that.

Man: I was worried. Where have you been?

*(The **Woman** shrugs.)*

Man: Have you been away?

Woman: Ha! Yeah! The Canaries!

*(The **Man** smiles at this. She smiles back.)*

Woman: Bernadette not with you?

Man: No. She's moved to Australia.

Woman: Oh.

Man: It seems to be the place to go.

Woman: I'd say Mam took that hard.

Man: Well it's very far away. Very hard to keep in touch. The time difference. The distance. Down under.

Woman: Yeah.

(Voices off – female – boisterous, "Whoooooooohooooooooooh!" Laughter.)

Woman: Did you have a party?

Man: For Bernie?

Woman: No for your birthday …

Man: Oh! Yeah. Yeah.

Woman: Yeah.

*(The **Woman** lifts a cigarette butt from the pavement and goes to light it. The **Man** fishes in his pocket and produces an old-fashioned gentleman's pipe.)*

Man: Here.

(She lights it.)

Woman: It smells like you.

Man: It's funny – but because it belonged to my da, I always think it smells like him.

(He watches her smoke.)

Woman: "I yam what I yam."

Man: Ha! That's … We used to …You'd never know it now but you were a very hungry baby. We never knew when to stop feeding you. And you'd cry and you'd cry. And we'd keep shovelling the food down you. And we'd look at you and say what's wrong? What's wrong? –

Woman: *(interrupting)* – I'm not coming with you.

Man: And your mother would be boiling and whizzing vegetables –

Woman: I'm not coming.

Man: And we'd say that you were like Popeye. Because if you could have squeezed cans open, like he did, and glugged the spinach down – you would have. Like Popeye.

(A voice off – female – drunk. "Don't come fucking near me, d'you hear me?" Footsteps.

*Silence. The **Man** and **Woman** regard each other.*

*The **Man** gets up. He takes the pipe from out of her hands.)*

Woman: Can I keep it?

Man: I don't think so.

(He kisses the **Woman** *on the forehead.)*

Man: It's precious, but it's not worth anything.

(He starts to walk away.)

Woman: Could you spare any cash?

(He stops.

He continues walking.

Ends.)

Light At The End Of The Tunnel

By Eleanor White

*A train station, night time. An **Intercom** crackles to life.*

Intercom: The 21:00 train to Limerick has been delayed by four minutes. Thank you for your patience.

Boy: It's funny how time passes, isn't it? Four minutes on Facebook feels like nothing. Four minutes of Biology class on a Monday morning lasts an eternity. Four minutes of dinner is all a teenage boy needs to clear his plate. But nothing lasts longer than waiting four minutes for a train to come.

Mother's Voice: Darling, come home. I'm sorry. Your father's sorry. He didn't mean it. We love you very much, you do know that. Very, very much.

Boy: This always seemed so easy, you know? And I guess it is. Well, I don't know. I don't know anything any more. I suppose I'll find out in four minutes.

Girl's Voice: I feel like I don't know you any more. I want to help you. I really, really like you. Hell, I might love you. I don't know. I know you feel the same, though. Or you used to. What changed?

Boy: I'm still the same person. I'm still me. I love chocolate and telly and the feel of grass underneath my bare feet and all of that sentimental shit. But I just – it's like the world's suffocating me, you know? I can't breathe.

Friend's Voice: You do my head in sometimes, do you know that? We're best friends, right? If you've got a problem, why don't you talk to me? Is it your parents? Is it her? Oh, for God's sake. Why can't you just tell me?

Intercom: The 21:00 train to Limerick will be here in two minutes.

Boy: Have you ever had a secret? I don't mean something like taking a fiver from your mum's purse. I mean something big. Something huge. Something that would destroy everything if it got out.

Father's Voice: I cannot believe this. How could you do this? To me? To your family?

Boy: So you keep it to yourself. Even though it kills you not to talk about it. Because anything is better than people finding out.

Father's Voice: You're a disgrace. From this moment on, you are no longer my son.

Boy: But say that someone finds out about your secret. That everyone finds out. And everything changes. What do you do then?

Father's Voice: You're disgusting.

Boy: Do you keep going? You can't keep going. Not like this.

Father's Voice: Fag.

Other Boy's Voice: It's okay. Everything will be okay. I love you. We'll run away together if we have to – somewhere far away where no one knows our names. It'll be okay, as long as we can be together. You're so beautiful when you cry. We'll get through this. I know we will.

You just have to be strong.

Boy: Being strong is hard. Too hard. And I can't do it anymore. I've been suffocated. I can't breathe.

Intercom: The 21:00 train to Limerick is approaching the station.

Mother's Voice: Come home –

Girl's Voice: What changed? –

Friend's Voice: For God's sake –

Father's Voice: Fag –

Other Boy's Voice: I love you –

(The sound of a train pulling into a station.

Boy *steps forward. A squeal of brakes. Blackout.)*

Naked Photographs Of My Mother

By Brendan Griffin

*Gerry, 30s, is in **Dillon's**, 30s, kitchen. **Gerry** is forlorn and is sitting at the kitchen table with his hands protectively over an envelope of photographs as **Dillon** brings two mugs of coffee.*

***Dillon** can't help laughing to himself, much to the displeasure of **Gerry**.*

Dillon: *(laughing)* Reinsulating the attic … I can imagine your surprise.

*(**Dillon** sits but again laughs inappropriately.)*

I do sympathise. I really do. Finding photographs of your mother …

Gerry: Just so as you understand why I came to you: you are leaving to Australia next week, and likely I may not see you for years; plus, you are a sad bastard, and I'm about the only person you can call half a friend, and you can't afford to lose me.

Dillon: I am to look at the photographs and tell you if they are, in general terms, the same as the one you saw.

Gerry: You glance at the photographs. You don't mention the woman by name, you just say, "Woman".

Dillon: What if there is a man?

Gerry: You say, "Man".

Dillon: Woman, man, got it.

Gerry: I will count them first.

*(**Gerry** lowers the envelope, fully out of his view, under the table, and counts, leafing the photographs.)*

Dillon: You really think I would want to steal a naked photograph of your late mother and father?

Gerry: What did I tell you?

Dillon: Woman, man.

Gerry: There are ten.

*(**Gerry** slides the envelope of photographs across the table towards **Dillon**, but retains possession.)*

Gerry: You glance. You do not refer to the woman as hot, sexy. You do not say, "Wow!" I will tell you when you can begin.

*(**Gerry** turns away needlessly to prevent seeing the photographs.)*

Gerry: *(beat)* Now.

*(**Dillon** takes the photographs out of the envelope.)*

Gerry: Let's make it quick.

*(**Dillon** begins looking at the photographs, impressed / taken aback.)*

Gerry: I said just glance.

Dillon: That's all I'm doing.

*(**Gerry** can't resist turning to watch **Dillon** viewing the photographs.)*

Gerry: Finish up.

*(**Dillon** finishes viewing the photographs.)*

Gerry: Put them back in the envelope.

*(**Dillon** returns the photographs to the envelope. **Gerry** puts out his hand and **Dillon** gives him the envelope. **Gerry** once again lowers the envelope under the table and recounts the photographs.)*

Dillon: Trust me, they are all there.

*(**Gerry** is satisfied that all the photographs are there.)*

Gerry: Well, are they all in the same mode?

Dillon: The good old Instamatic – that's all they had back then.

Gerry: Does the man make an appearance?

Dillon: No.

*(**Gerry** is visibly relieved.)*

Dillon: You just saw the first one, she, the woman, is lying across the bed?

Gerry: I'm trying to forget that I saw anything at all. I instantly shoved them back in the envelope.

Dillon: They are mostly of the woman lying on the bed, in the bedroom, various poses.

Gerry: I don't need to know any detail.

Dillon: They were well taken.

Gerry: They were not all taken in the bedroom then?

Dillon: You said you did not want detail. It is best that way.

*(**Gerry** wrestles with knowing.)*

Gerry: Where were the others taken?

Dillon: In the sitting room. It is Christmas time. The tree is in the background.

Gerry: *(dismissing)* So why was it best I did not know that?

*(**Dillon** does not reply.)*

Gerry: *(demanding)* Why?

Dillon: She is sitting on your ten-speed racer. You loved that bike. You still have it, don't you?

(Beat.)

She is smiling in every single photograph. She was happy.

And she was more than hot, the woman was beautiful.

(The End)

The Cost Of Your Forgetting

By Henry Martin

*A nightclub. Some music. **Tim** is wearing a T-shirt with a skeleton outline on it: ribcage, clavicle, etc. **Gabby** approaches.*

Gabby: There aren't any skeletons in your closet then?

Tim: What's that?

Gabby: Skeletons in your closet.

Tim: I don't have a closet.

Gabby: I was referring to your T-shirt.

Tim: Oh. (*looks*) Yeah. That's funny.

Gabby: My name's Gabby.

Tim: My name is Caesar salad. My mom was a crouton, and my dad was an iceberg lettuce.

Gabby: What?

Tim: I heard it on the radio once. I thought it was funny. It's good to break the ice. I'm a bit of a loser – that's my skeleton. What's yours?

Gabby: I wrote a book once.

Tim: Do I know it?

Gabby: The movie version starred Clarke Gable and Vivien Leigh.

Tim: Never heard of it.

Gabby: So what kind of girls do you like?

Tim: I'm not looking right now. The last one did this (*points to his T-shirt.*)

Gabby: You're still here, right?

Tim: What do you look for?

Gabby: You mean generally, or tonight?

Tim: Whichever.

Gabby: Abs. I look for good abs.

Tim: (*grabbing his belly*) Oh, well.

Gabby: I said abs are what I look for – not what I get.

Also, someone with tough skin.

Tim: Why?

Gabby: I bite.

Tim: Ok, then.

Gabby: No, really. I'm looking for a relationship too – after the sex.

Tim: You haven't even bought me a drink yet. I do have some standards.

Gabby: Do you believe in love at first sight?

Tim: No.

Gabby: Do you believe that I could need you so much, I could eat you. Like actually cut your finger off, fry it and eat it?

Tim: It's not one of *those* clubs is it?

Gabby: I'm going to kiss you.

Tim: No.

Gabby: If I can guess three things correctly about you, I'm going to kiss you.

Tim: No. Ok. Maybe.

Gabby: When you were twelve you were in a minor car crash coming down the Galtee Mountains. You bumped your head, and demanded that the paramedic give you an eye-patch, though your eye was actually fine. Your father told you not to tempt fate.

Tim: Who are you?

Gabby: You had a fight with your girlfriend when you were on holiday in Milan. Then you went to a club alone. You met a girl called Gabrielle. She looked into your eyes like this. (**Gabby** *looks into his eyes.*) She took you home. In the morning you felt regret. You told Gabrielle the whole story. She felt sorry for you. She knew what it was like; the way we try and hurt each other but only get hurt doing it. You said:

Tim: "I want to forget about this. I want it erased from my memory."

Gabby: (*at the same time*) "I want to forget about this. I want it erased from my memory." Gabrielle said, "All things come at a price". But you were so sure that you and your girlfriend …

Tim: (*distant*) Caoimhe.

Gabby: ... so sure that you and her were meant to be together ...

Tim: "Just make me forget."

Gabby: "I'll make you forget, but if you *or* Caoimhe ever cheat on each other, I will come and claim the cost of your forgetting."

(*Sad*) And so you forgot. "And it's all just a little bit of history repeating." I think I get to kiss you now.

(***Gabby*** *leans in to kiss him.*)

Tim: No.

(***Gabby*** *stops.*)

I never forgot. I've never cheated on her.

(*Moving closer.*)

Gabby: The deal was made for both of you. I'm sorry, Tim. It was Caoimhe who moved on.

Tim: I.

Gabby: Don't run.

Tim: I.

Gabby: It will only be awkward.

Tim: I don't believe you.

(***Gabby*** *leans in and kisses* ***Tim***. *She puts her hand on* ***Tim's*** *T-shirt, and pulls away a rib. Both look at the rib, covered in blood.*)

Tim: That hurt.

(*Tim* *starts bleeding.* *Gabby* *is tender, and upset by her own actions.*)

Gabby: I really did like your T-shirt.

I'm sorry.

I Stand Here Before You

By Tom Swift

*A **Politician** enters, followed by a **Translator**. The **Politician** goes to a podium, scans the audience and clears his throat. The **Translator** takes up position at a microphone, but the **Politician** doesn't seem aware his words are being translated.*

Politician: I stand here before you. An ordinary man. A people person.

Translator: I understand your deepest prejudices. Like you, my childhood was not a happy one.

Politician: *(abandoning the podium)* I have no time for fancy talk. I am a straight talker.

Translator: Intellectuals disgust me.

Politician: And I want to get the job done. I want to get the job done, for you, for this country.

Translator: The roads of my constituency are smooth and wide. My home town has a new Olympic-size swimming pool.

Politician: During the course of this campaign I've been speaking to a lot of people, ordinary people.

Translator: The tinted windows of my limousine protect me from reality and harmful UV rays.

Politician: Because I want to hear what you have to say. And because I believe the people of this country of ours are a great people, a proud people.

Translator: You disgust me.

Politician: That's why I want you to come out next Friday and do what's right for the country, do what's right for your families and future generations to come.

Translator: This is a game I play.

Politician: Now I'm happy to take any questions.

Translator: Shoot.

(A **Man** stands up in the audience, his arm raised.)

Man: People say you have no ideas, that you don't believe in anything, they say all you care about is self-promotion and money. And they're dead right. You're just an ordinary person, like me. This country needs leaders like you. Men, ordinary men – pint-drinkers, compulsive gamblers. So, if you're telling me that you're getting things done and if my kids can swim in an Olympic-size swimming pool ... Well then all that crowd with their bitching and complaining would want to just get out of your way and let you get on with the job, whatever it is you're doing!

(Wild applause and cheers. The **Politician** waves to the crowd and exits.

Some years later ... The **Politician** enters to the sound of a tense whispers, camera flashes and occasional boos. He goes to the podium, scans the audience, clears his throat.)

Politician: I stand here before you. An ordinary man. I'm only human.

Translator: I told you, my childhood was unhappy.

Politician: So, I'll get straight to the point.

Translator: I want to murder you.

Man: Boo ... Boo ... !

Politician: *(emotional)* Yes. I did what I did ... but it was a difficult time for me, personally.

Translator: My heart is a glacier.

Politician: So you can think what you like. But I want to say this ...

Translator: I have a limousine.

Politician: I want to say this: I never did anything wrong, ever.

Translator: Grown men meeting in darkened car parks is not a crime.

Man: Liar! You're a dirty liar!

Politician: It's all accounted for ... I got lucky on the gee-gees!

Translator: I've lost him surely.

Man: Look what you've done to us! To think some people were ever taken in by your waffle. You have no ideas, you don't believe in anything, all you care about is self-promotion and money. I'll say it again – This country has had enough of leaders like you, enough of all your crowd. I'm out of a job, I haven't even the price of a pint, and that Olympic-size swimming pool is leaking like a sieve!

*(The **Politician** bows his head for a moment.)*

Politician: The people have spoken. I hear you. I did my best. I did my best, but there you go. That's democracy for you.

Translator: Why don't you kill yourselves?

*(The **Politician** leaves, waving with a fixed expression. A pause. The **Translator** scans the audience, waiting. Finally the **Man** walks down from the audience and approaches the podium. He scans the audience, clears his throat.)*

Man: I stand here before you. An ordinary man. A people person.

Positive Protest

By Christine McKeon

Two actors enter stage and discuss protest and the idea of protesting the lack of protest. That the people of Ireland have been drawn into looking at the now and how to survive it rather than looking forward and a better society. The general Irish people do not have a history of philosophy. Favourite philosophers are not high in popularity charts. The actors encourage the audience not only to think blue sky thinking but to share this idea with others.

A piece of card and a pen will be pre-positioned under each chair in the audience. An actor asks the audience to pick up the paper and pen and write a word or sentence (not a novel) of a positive idea they would like to see in the Ireland of five years in the future. They then pass the card to the person in front of them (or alternatively look for someone in the audience that they do not know), in effect passing on the idea.

The actor asks 10 random people to read out the ideas on the cards in front of them.

These ideas are dictated to the other actor, who writes a letter addressed to President Higgins as suggestions from Tiny Plays for a better society. It is then placed in an envelope and a courier (could be actor #3) takes it to be delivered to the Áras.

Each night the letter will obviously be different.

The Caring

By Pauline McLynn

*The action takes place in a hospital corridor. I suggest the audience
'be' the wall behind the chairs and bed on which the action takes
place for optimum view of the proceedings. In tone, the play should
shift from funny to poignant and funny-poignant, as necessary,
with JAY intended to be a drunk who is as ridiculous as selfish
drunks are, but who also manages to do a good thing.*

*The constant soundtrack throughout the piece is of a busy, over-
worked hospital – footsteps, shouts, paging staff and visitors, etc.
The corridor should have as much human traffic as possible passing by – same actors with different coats and so on, some brisk,
some running, never stopping – BUSY. A note is that medical
people are very adept at not getting stopped when they don't want
to be. None of the ones in the play are bad or nasty, they're just
hassled and overworked, spread too thinly.*

*We see a hospital trolley bed, behind a screen. On either side are
chairs along the 'wall' for visitors to sit on. An OLD MAN is in
the bed, ignored.*

*Over the din of the hospital we hear, then see, the arrival of a new
patient/casualty.*

Jay: Fucksake, I can WALK, I'm not a cripple, you know. I just banged me head is all.

Nurse: This is a precaution. You might fall again and hurt yourself even more. You *are* still a bit drunk, Mr Hanlon.

Jay: Wish I fuckin' was. Wouldn't have the pain in me head till tomorrow then. Wouldn't mind, I was only leaning over to have a slash then BOOM the wall fuckin' ups and smacks me. No warning, just BOOF! (*He sniffs his clothes.*) Any chance of a change? When the wall attacked me, I kinda fell into the mess ... (*He pats his pockets.*) robbin' fuckin' CUNTS took me phone n' all. Has no one any respect for human life any more?

He is wheeled over to the chairs and helped out and into one. His head is bandaged, he is very dishevelled and dirty and beaten-up looking – looks the sort of rough you'd cross the road to avoid.

Jay: Where's me bed?

Nurse: This is it, I'm afraid. Probably just as well. We don't want you nodding off in case you have concussion.

Jay: (*who is indeed still drunk, seizes on this*) Is me life in danger, Miss? Could I, like, fall into a coma, and die, or be a vegetable if I wake up and don't die, until I die – be a vegetable that is ...?

Nurse: Please just wait here, Mr Hanlon, we'll keep an eye on you and I'm sure you can go home in the morning

She makes to go, clearly busy.

Jay: Why can't I have that bed there?

Nurse: Because it's occupied.

Jay: I matter too, you know. I'm not well. (*He is suddenly very sorry for himself, as drunk people often are.*) I didn't ask for this grief, you know. And I'm not an animal to be abandoned in a strange corridor on a feckin' CHAIR when I should be in a bed. This country is gone to hell.

The NURSE is making her exit now.

Nurse: There are some very ill people here so, please, keep your voice down, Mr Hanlon.

Jay: *I'm* fuckin' ill. I'm one of the walkin' fuckin' wounded right now!

He tries to settle or get comfortable on one and all of the chairs (Have fun with this, make a little comedy routine of it and feel free to say whatever comes of it.)

Suddenly there is a loud and anguished cry from the OLD MAN in the trolley bed. It frightens the shit out of JAY. After a time, moaning becomes crying and JAY goes to investigate.

Jay: Ah, don't cry, man. You're grand. Sure, aren't you in the right place for … whatever it is you're here for. I banged me head. Fuckin' sore, I don't mind tellin' ya. An' all I got was this turban to fix it. No tablets, nothin'. Not even a bed. Actually I'm lyin' to ya, they gave me a tetanus shot, or maybe it was rabies, I dunno, there's a lot of new diseases flyin' around these days.

Would you like to sit up, would that help? Nothin' much to see, mind, but a change is as good as a rest an' all that?

He helps the OLD MAN up into a seated position.

Jay: I'll say one thing for them, they're scabby cunts with the pills an' all but they give you plenty of pillows. No shortage of them, that's for sure. Shame there's no buzz off a pillow, or you'd be laughin' all the way to wherever you need to go.

The OLD MAN grabs his hand and won't let go. JAY really doesn't know how to handle this stranger or get away from him. The OLD MAN is muttering.

Jay: Don't be mad. Sure there's nothing to be afraid of. Aren't you goin' to be well looked after here … and all fixed up … and all.

He looks around for help but can't get anyone to stop or take notice.

Jay: Is there any chance of a bit of attention here? Huh? Eh, sick people here? Help? Anyone?

The OLD MAN now has a very good hold on JAY and it's as easy to sit on the bed with him as try to escape, so he does.

Jay: You've a fair aul' grip on ya all the same, I'll tell ya that for nothin'. Someone'll be along any minute now and we'll be sorted.

Bit of a silence, except for the din of the hospital.

Jay: Have you family?

No answer from the OLD MAN

Jay: Yeah, me neither. Well, I do but I might as well not have, if you know what I mean. I'm Jay, what's your name?

The OLD MAN mutters his answer and again JAY has to lean in to hear it.

Jay: Michael, right. Grand. Nice an', I dunno, *sturdy* of a name. (*then loudly to the air*) Still waitin' on some help here. Sick people an' all.

The OLD MAN is sobbing and gasping for breath again.

Jay: Ah now, you're only stressin' yourself. Relax. I have ya now, you'll be grand. (*He means these words to be helpful* *but clearly there's no way he can be of much help to a very ill old man and he knows it. Then ...)*

I know. We should pass the time, that's the ticket for this place. My gran, the only one I liked in me family, the only decent skin to come out of our lot, she loved a singsong. How about we try that?

The OLD MAN is at least calmer now, raspy breathing though, fading a bit?

JAY tries to sing, haltingly, not sure of the words to anything.

Jay: I think I should do a medley, you know? Safest bet, really. Bit of everything, you know?

Are you right there, Michael, are you right?

Do you think that we'll be home before the night?

Sure it all depends on whether the auld engine holds together,

And it might now, Michael, so it might.

How much is that doggie in the window?

The one with the waggedy tail.

How much is that doggie in the window?

I do hope that doggie's for sale.

Two drifters off to see the world.

There's such a lot of world to see.

We're after the same rainbow's end,

Waiting round the bend,

My huckleberry friend,

Moon River and me.

The OLD MAN has passed away during this. People still go by, without noticing. JAY gently rests him down and he looks like he's sleeping peacefully now. He leaves the screen slightly back as he goes and sits in his chair, his back to us (obviously). A MEDIC passes and smiles at JAY, then notices the screen and puts it back into place to cover up the OLD MAN.

Medic: Happy out, huh? The old guy.

Jay: (without looking at the MEDIC) His name is Michael. Yeah, he's happy out all right.

We fade as the toing and froing continues on the corridor and the sound of the hospital's work continues to be heard.

Life In 2 Syllables

By Mike Finn

*Three actors play three characters, **Man**, **Woman** and **Guy**. This is **Man's** story – **Woman** and **Guy** help him tell it.*

Man: Life in ...

Woman: Two syll ...

Guy: A-bells.

(Pause.)

Woman: Oh God.

Guy: Push hard!

Woman: I can't!

Guy: You can!

Woman: The pain!

Guy: Breathe in!

Woman: I am!

Guy: Breathe out!

Woman: Shut up!

Guy: Come on!

Woman: Get lost!

Guy: A head!

Woman: Thank Christ!

Guy: A boy!

Woman: Don't care!

Man: Boo hoo!

Guy: My son.

Man: Boo hoo!

Guy: I'm Dad.

Man: *(raspberries)* Bubbb bubbbb.

Guy: Oh shit!

(Pause.)

Man: I'm John.

Guy: I know.

Man: I'm two.

Guy: I know.

Man: I'm John.

Guy: I know.

Man: I'm two.

Guy: I know!

Man: I'm John.

Guy: Shut up!

Man: Ok.

(Pause.)

Woman: You're six.

Man: Hurray!

Guy: You're twelve.

Man: So what?

Woman: Stay home.

Man: Get lost.

(Pause.)

Man: You're cute.

Woman: You too.

Man: I'm drunk.

Woman: Me too.

Man: Do you … ?

Woman: Do I … ?

Man: You know … ?

Woman: I do.

Man: With who?

Woman: A few.

Man: Me too.

Woman: With who?

Man: A few.

Woman: Like who?

Man: Well … none.

Woman: You're cute!

Man: I'm pissed.

Woman: Me too.

(Pause.)

Man: Will we?

Woman: Why not?

(Pause.)

Man: Oh God!

Woman: That's nice.

Man: Oh God!

Woman: Slow down.

Man: Oh God!

Woman: Pull out!

Man: Oh God!

Woman: PULL OUT!

Man: Too late.

Woman: Oh God.

(Pause.)

Woman: Ring ring.

Guy: For you.

Man: For me?

Guy: Some girl.

(Pause.)

Man: You're what?

Woman: You know ...

Man: Oh God!

Woman: I know.

Man: Am I?

Woman: Of course.

Man: What now?

Woman: Don't know.

(Pause.)

Man: Should we?

Woman: I guess.

Man: Will you?

Woman: I will.

Man: *(humming 'Here Comes The Bride')* Dum dum ...

Woman: *(humming)* De dum ...

Man: *(humming)* Dum dum ...

Woman: De dum.

Guy: Do you?

Man: I do.

Guy: Do you?

Woman: I do.

Guy: You may.

(**Man** *and* **Woman** *kiss.*)

Man, Woman & Guy: Hurray!

(*They throw confetti in the air. Pause.*)

Woman: Oh God.

Man: Push hard!

Woman: I can't!

Man: You can!

Woman: The pain!

Man: Breath in!

Woman: I am!

Man: Breath out!

Woman: Shut up!

Man: Come on!

Woman: Shag off!

Man: A head!

Woman: Thank Christ!

Man: A girl!

Woman: Don't care!

Guy: Boo hoo!

Man: So small.

Guy: Boo hoo!

Man: So cute!

Guy: Boo hoo!

Man: I'm Dad.

Guy: Boo hoo!

Man: Boo hoo!

(*Pause.*)

Man: Knock knock.

Guy: Come in.

Man: Thank you.

Guy: Sit down.

Man: OK.

Guy: Now then.

Man: CV.

Guy: I see.

Man: Well then?

Guy: You'll do.

Man: How much?

Guy: Not much.

Man: Ok.

(*Pause.*)

Man: She's six.

Woman: I know.

Man: She's ten.

Woman: I know.

Man: A teen.

Woman: I know.

Man: She's what?

Woman: You know ...

Man: My God!

Woman: I know.

Man: With who?

Woman: Don't know.

Man: My God!

(Pause.)

Man: Knock knock.

Guy: Come in.

Man: You called.

Guy: Bad news.

Man: Like what?

Guy: You're fired.

Man: I'm what?

Guy: You're fired.

Man: You can't.

Guy: Just did.

Man: I'm broke.

Guy: Don't care.

Man: What next?

(Pause.)

Woman: Sit down.

Man: What's wrong?

Woman: Your dad.

Man: What now?

(Pause.)

Woman: He's dead.

(Long pause.)

Man: Ok.

(Pause.)

Woman: Oh Dad!

Man: Push hard!

Woman: I can't!

Man: You can!

Woman: The pain!

Man: Breath in!

Woman: I am!

Man: Breath out!

Woman: Shut up!

Man: Come on!

Woman: Piss off!

Man: A head!

Woman: Thank Christ!

Man: A boy!

Woman: Don't care!

Guy: Boo hoo!

Man: He's huge!

Woman: I know!

Guy: Boo hoo!

Man: He's cute!

Guy: Boo hoo!

Man: Grandson!

Guy: Bo hoo!

Man: Grandad!

Guy: Boo hoo!

Man: Boo hoo!

(Pause.)

Man: Knock knock.

Guy: Come in.

Man: Thank you.

Guy: Sit down.

Man: CV.

Guy: Too old.

Man: I'm not.

Guy: 'Fraid so.

Man: I'm not.

Guy: Goodbye.

(Pause.)

Woman: What's this?

Man: Don't know.

Woman: Don't lie.

Man: I'm not.

Woman: Who's she?

Man: A friend.

Woman: Get out!

(Pause.)

Guy: Hey, you.

Man: Who me?

Guy: Drink up.

Man: One more.

Guy: No way.

Man: Fuck you!

Guy: Get out!

Man: Ok.

(Pause.)

Guy: Who's next?

Man: That's me.

Guy: Come in.

Man: What's up?

Guy: Your heart.

Man: How bad?

Guy: Not good.

Man: How long?

Guy: Not much.

(Pause.)

Man: Ok.

(Pause.)

Guy: Bip bip.

(Pause.)

Guy: Bip bip.

(Pause.)

Guy: Bip bip.

Woman: Hi Dad.

Man: Princess.

Guy: Bip bip.

Man: Where's Mum?

Woman: Not here.

Guy: Bip bip.

Woman: What's that?

Man: Machine.

Guy: Bip bip.

Woman: Don't go.

Man: Can't stay.

Guy: Bip bip.

Man: Don't cry.

Woman: Hang on.

Man: I can't!

Woman: You can!

Man: The pain!

Woman: Breath in!

Man: I am!

Woman: Breath out!

Guy: Bip bip.

Man: Shut up.

(Pause.)

Guy: Grandad?

Man: Yes, pet.

Guy: Love you.

Man: I know.

(Pause.)

Woman: Bip bip.

(Pause.)

Guy: Bip bip.

(Pause.)

Man: Bip.

*(Pause. Long silence.
The end.)*

Slanesman

By Colum McCann

*Lights up. In the centre of the otherwise bare stage, man, **C**, sits at an empty work desk, his feet propped up, looking out at the audience. He is dressed in a contemporary businessman's suit, open tie, polished shoes. **B**, a woman, comes out stage left. she is wearing a long, flowing, humble dress. She is redolent of more ancient times. **A**, an older man who has worked the bogs, comes out stage right: traditional Irish clothing, sleeves rolled up. They stand to the side of the desk, move around it and behind it. It should be odd — the clash of the old and the new. All the time **C** remains at his desk.*

A: It's an ancient story.

B: They're all ancient stories.

A: He was good with a slean. He could dig the height of a man.

B: He was always there, sculpting the earth.

A: We watched him.

B: A joy to watch.

A: First there was the scraw.

B: You used a scraitheog.

C: When you cut through the scraw it's like opening up the top of your skull.

B: It's a long blade on a piece of sally.

A: Then there's the white turf.

C: It gives way quickly to the proper dark.

A: Sometimes he'd dig the length of a sunrise before he could harvest.

B: We'd bring him milk and fresh bread from the oven.

A: There were slanesmen, wheelers, barrowmen, stackers.

B: The sod was tossed to the waiting barrowmen.

A: Spread out on the cutaway.

B: To be stacked and dried.

C: You could tell the time of day from the length of ditch shadows.

B: The sods became heavier the more the day went on.

A: More water in the cut.

B: A man would time his muscle to the sunset.

A: You'd see the long dresses traipsing across the green sedge.

B: Flasks of tea in the late afternoon. Our children coming home from school. Their arms stretched wide. Making airplanes across the land. Like they were already leaving.

A: If the cut was deep enough, they'd lower baskets.

B: Down there –

C: What we wanted –

Slanesman – Colum McCann

A: The deeper you go –

C: Something beyond soil.

B: – the more water seeps in the hole.

C: The carcass of an elk. A scroll. A chalice. That's what we wanted. As the years went on. Chalices.

A: A sudden burst of water.

B: … it filled the ditch.

A: He was so tired –

B: There were no platforms –

A: he couldn't climb out

B: Too deep down.

A: He scrambled at the edges

B: Laid the slean across the ditch –

A: – it snapped when he grabbed it.

A: They had no ropes.

B: We could hear him from a distance.

C: The quiet drip and drizzle of a dream.

A: My son.

B: Our boy. A slanesman.

A: We could hear him. He was still calling –

B: – from underground. There he was. Calling out for us.

A: Sometimes I think I'm still down there with him

B: – digging.